Mary Mapes Dodge

A New Baby World

Stories, Rhymes, And Pictures for Little Folks

Mary Mapes Dodge

A New Baby World
Stories, Rhymes, And Pictures for Little Folks

ISBN/EAN: 9783744724326

Printed in Europe, USA, Canada, Australia, Japan

Cover: Foto ©Thomas Meinert / pixelio.de

More available books at **www.hansebooks.com**

A NEW
BABY WORLD

STORIES, RHYMES, AND PICTURES

FOR LITTLE FOLKS

COMPILED FROM ST. NICHOLAS

BY MARY MAPES DODGE

PUBLISHERS' NOTE TO PARENTS.

THE remarkable success of BABY WORLD in its various editions here naturally results in a fresh compilation of similar selections from ST. NICHOLAS, in which only the favorite and most popular contributions to the earlier editions have been retained. Fully three-fourths of the present volume is made up of material newly selected from recent volumes of the magazine. Pictorially, and in other respects, this NEW BABY WORLD claims to be an advance upon its predecessors.

> To the Babies, Large and Small;
> To the Children, One and All.

Baby world is a busy world,—
    Is n't it, children dear?
Full of sights you must see and know,
    Full of sounds you must hear,
Full of things that "you must not touch,"
    Full of puzzles both great and small,
Full of people you love so much!
    And, oh, such a pleasant world after all!

That is *your* Baby world, spick and span;
And here is a book on the self-same plan.
Perhaps you 'll find it alive and glad
As any world you ever have had.
There are dogs and horses, kittens, birds,
And songs and stories and happy words;
And skates and hooples, sleds and toys;
Merry girls and frolicsome boys,
Flowers and trees, and landscapes fair;—
Why, you 'll think you are out in the open air!
Well from its pages may sunlight shine,
For Baby world floats in a light divine.

Yes, Baby world is full of joy,
    Full of merriment, love and light;
And you, my girl! and you, my boy!
    Can help to keep it fair and bright.
Pleasant speech and a cheerful face,
    A willing heart and gentle grace,
A love of God, and a soul that is true,—
    These are the light that can shine from you.

Glad Baby world! bright Baby world!
With joy like a great blue sky unfurled!
With your Slumberland, Fairyland, Storyland, all;
Your stars so great, and your clouds so small;
Your torrents of tears that are gone in the sun,
Your mountains of trouble that vanish in fun,—
What could we big folk do without you?
We with our sweet loving trouble about you?
Why, we could do nothing but cry all day
If Baby world ever should pass away!

Then up and around us, ye little folk! Look!
There's a world of your own in this beautiful book.
And just as long as you please you may stay;
And whenever you please you may scamper away.

                                          M. M. D.

"SUCH A COMICAL WORLD!"

CONTENTS.

		PAGE
ALICE'S SUPPER	Laura E. Richards	145
"ALL ABOARD FOR THE MOON!" Picture, drawn by	V. Nehlig	79
"ANNA, MANA, MONA, MIKE"	Lee Carter	59
ANIMALS OF BERNE, THE	Pauline King	147
AT RECESS. THE DANCING BEAR. Picture, drawn by	N. M. Walcott	133
BABY'S JOURNEY	Laura E. Richards	95
BABY'S SUNNY CORNER, THE. Picture, drawn by	Mary Hallock Foote	94
BALLAD OF A RUNAWAY DONKEY, THE	Emilie Poulsson	110, 111
BARGAINS FOR SCHOLARS	Anna M. Pratt	69
BELL-RINGERS, THE	M. M. D.	134, 135
BENNY AND HIS BOATS	M. L. B. Branch	186, 187
BERTIE'S FIRST DAY AT SCHOOL	S. Mary Norton	6
BEST TREE, THE	Janet Sanderson	196, 197
BICYCLE SONG	Harriet Prescott Spofford	89
BIG BOOBOO AND THE LITTLE BOOBOO, THE	Gertrude Smith	1
BINGO, BUSTER AND BEAU	James Harvey Smith	58
BOBOLINK AND THE CHICK-A-DEE, THE	M. Ella Preston	127
BOB'S WAY	Tudor Jenks	74
BOY AND THE TOOT, THE	M. S.	73
BRIGHT SIDE, THE	Algernon Tassin	112
BROTHERS, THE	Agnes Lewis Mitchill	65
BUMBLE-BEE, THE	Laura E. Richards	146
BUMBLE-BEE AND THE GRASS-HOPPER, THE		165
BUMBLE-BEES, THE	Nell K. McElh ne	189
"BUT THEN, IN SUMMER, YOU CAN PLAY ON THE BEACH!" Picture, drawn by	M. O. Kobbé	28
CAMPING	Agnes Lewis Mitchill	50
CAT AND RAT THAT LIVED IN AN OVEN, THE	Margaret R. Gorseline	86
CAT-PRANKS. Pictures, drawn by	J. G. Francis	123
CHUMS. Picture, drawn by	J. H. Dolph	facing page 1

XI

		PAGE
CIRCUS ELEPHANTS HAVING A GOOD TIME BY THEMSELVES. } Picture . . . . *J. Carter Beard*		180
CIRCUS ELEPHANT'S SATURDAY NIGHT BATH, THE. Picture		180
CITY CHILD, THE . . . . *Alfred Tennyson*		184
CLOSE OF THE DAY, THE . . . . *M. L. V.*		65
CONCEITED MOUSE, THE . . . . *Ella Foster Case*		16, 17
CRADLE SONG . . . . *Margaret Johnson*		185
CUP OF TEA, A . . . . *E. L. Sylvester*		57
DEAD DOLL, THE . . . . *Margaret Vandegrift*		182
"DEAR ME, LUCY ANN, IF YOU'RE NOT MORE CAREFULLER OF YOURSELF, YOU'LL NOT LAST TILL CHRISTMAS!" } Picture, drawn by . . *Aug. D. Turner*		11
DIFFERENCE BETWEEN UP AND DOWN, THE. Picture, drawn by *H. Stull*		103
DOLLS' CHRISTMAS DINNER, THE. Picture, drawn by . . . . *V. Pérard*		9
DON'T YOU THINK THAT WINTER'S PLEASANTER THAN ALL? . . . . } Picture, drawn by . . . *John Bolles*		27
DORA AND HER RING . . . . *Horatio Nelson Powers*		10
DOT AND THE NEW MOON . . . . *Anna E. Langdon*		190
DOWN IN THE MEADOW . . . . *Ruth Hall*		184
EARLY AND LATE . . . . *W. S. Reed*		87
EIGHT GOOD THINGS ABOUT DOBBIN . . . . *M. M. D.*		142
ELEPHANT AND THE GIRAFFE, THE . . . . *Charlotte Osgood Carter*		31
ENOUGH FOR TWO. Picture, drawn by . . . . *J. Carter Beard*		93
FAIRY GODMOTHER, A . . . . *Mary Bradley*		188
FALL TO THE KNEES, A . . . . *Mae St. John Bramhall*		12
FAMILY DRIVE, A . . . . *Stephen Smith*		72
FAMILY DRUM CORPS, A . . . . *Malcolm Douglas,*		191,192,193
FAMILY GROUP, A. Picture		49
FERN-SEED . . . . *Agnes Lewis Mitchill*		10
FIELDS, THE . . . . *Thomas Tapper*		157
FOUR LITTLE PIGS . . . . *Malcolm Douglas*		105
FOURTH OF JULY STORY, A		56
FROG'S FOURTH OF JULY, THE . . . . *Mary A. L. Eastman*		29
FROM "FIDO" . . . . *Tudor Jenks*		66
GENUINE MOTHER GOOSE, A . . . . *Alfred Brennan*		164
GINGER-BREAD BOY, THE		96
GOING TO THE MOON		78
GOOD BOY BRIGADE, THE. Picture		98
GOOD FRIENDS		76, 77, 78
GOOD-NIGHT. Decorative Design . . . . *Albertine Randall Wheelan*		200

		PAGE
"Go 'Way! Go 'Way! They 're Flowers!" Picture, drawn by	*George Varian*	116
Grandmama	*Helen Hopkins*	113
Grandma's Nap	*M. M. D.*	82, 83, 84
Granger Grind and Farmer Mellow	*John Bennett*	148, 149
Great Bicycle Race at Grasshoppertown. Pictures, drawn by	*I. W. Taber*	172, 173
Greedy Toad	*Eliza S. Turner*	189
Grumpity Man, The	*Frank H. Sweet*	30
Halloa, Old Scuttle!		118
Ho, for the Christmas Tree! No One but the Baby May Peep. } Picture, drawn by	*George Varian*	64
How Curious!	*Tudor Jenks*	59
How Did She Know?	*Caroline Evans*	88
How Johnny Got a Gun	*H. A. Ogden*	60, 61
Howlery, Growlery Room, The	*Laura E. Richards*	18
How Rob Counted the Stars		102
How the Slide Was Spoiled	*Tudor Jenks*	120
How They Ride	*Eva L. Carson*	114, 115
"If Wishes Were Horses, then Beggars Would Ride" } Picture	*Kate Robertson*	148
If You 're Good	*James Courtney Challiss,*	198
I Had a Little Row Boat	*Cornelia Redmond*	121
Imaginary Case, An	*E. L. Sylvester*	21
In Top Time	*Henry Reeves*	131
In Japan	*Juliet Wilbor Tompkins*	171
Is n't It Queer?	*Mrs. H. M. Greenleaf*	142
"I 've Bringed You a Little Dolly, Bossy" } Picture, drawn by	*J. C. Bridgman*	143
Jingles	*John Kendrick Bangs*	175
Kettle, The	*Laura E. Richards*	68
Kite Time. Picture		85
Kittens' Picnic, The	*Tudor Jenks*	108, 109
Land of Noddy, The	*Rossiter Johnson*	183
Lion Met a Little Boy, A	*M. M. D.*	54, 55
Little Bertie	*M. M. D.*	129
Little Boy Named Johnny, A	*Cornelia Redmond*	21
Little Elf, The	*John Kendrick Bangs*	15
Little Man of Morrisburg, The	*William Wye Smith*	8
Little Mischief	*M. M. D.*	70, 71
Little Mr. By-and-By	*Clinton Scollard*	153
Little Peri-Winkle		107

		PAGE
LITTLE PET PUG AT THE CIRCUS, THE	*Tudor Jenks*	22, 23
LITTLE RED HEN	*Eudora S. Bumstead*	90, 91
LITTLE TOMMY TRIM	*Mary Elizabeth Stone*	12
"LITTLE TOMMY TUCKER, SING FOR YOUR SUPPER." Picture		146
"LOOK OUT, THERE!" Picture, from a carving by	*Joseph Lauber*	177
LOST HOURS	*Sydney Dayre*	66
MARCH—AND APRIL. Pictures		112, 113
MAY-TIME IN THE COUNTRY. Picture, drawn by	*Mary Hallock Foote*	156
MERRY CHRISTMAS	*Charlotte Brewster Jordan*	195
MIDNIGHT EXPRESS, THE. Picture, drawn by	*Culmer Barnes*	98
MISS LILYWHITE'S PARTY	*George Cooper*	9
MOON MUST LOVE ME VERY MUCH, THE	*Frederick B. Opper*	25
MR. ELEPHANT RINGING THE BELL FOR DINNER } Picture, drawn by	*J. C. Beard*	7
MY CHOICE	*Delia Hart Stone*	30
MY LADY IS EATING HER MUSH	*M. F. Butts*	127
MY TINY DAUGHTER DOLLY	*Dorothea Lummis*	13
NEEDLE, THE	*Laura E. Richards*	166
NEW MOTHER GOOSE JINGLE, A	*Dorothy G. Rice*	194
NEW MOTHER GOOSE RHYMES	*Dorothy G. Rice*	4, 5
NORSE LULLABY, A	*M. L. Van Vorst*	136
"NOW" AND "WAITAWHILE"	*Nixon Waterman*	124
NUMBER ONE	*Charles R. Talbot*	119
"OH, MR. FAIRY, PLEASE"	*Wilfrid Wilson Gibson*	151
OLD MAN BY THE GATE, THE	*Thomas S. Collier*	84
ONE DAY AN ANT WENT TO VISIT HER NEIGHBOR	*M. L. Van Vorst*	102
ON THE FERRY		49
ON THE ROAD TO LONDON TOWN	*E. M. Winston*	190
OWL, THE EEL, AND THE WARMING-PAN, THE	*Laura E. Richards*	107
PAINTING A CARD FOR MOTHER'S BIRTHDAY. Picture	*Frederick Dielman*	124
PERFECT GENTLEMAN, A. Picture, drawn by	*J. H. Dolph*	179
PICTURE, THE	*Mary Mapes Dodge*	199
POLITE OWL, A		13
"POOR LITTLE LAMB HAS BEEN RUNNING TOO HARD! THE" } Picture	*Mary Hallock Foote*	137
POPULAR POPLAR TREE, THE	*Blanche Willis Howard*	163
PRACTISING SONG	*Laura E. Richards*	155
PROBLEM IN THREES, A	*Eudora S. Bumstead*	57
PUNKYDOODLE AND JOLLAPIN	*Laura E. Richards*	107
PUSSY AND THE TURTLE	*M. M. D.*	158, 159

			PAGE
Pussy and her Elephant	. . . .	*Hannah Moore Johnson,*	52, 53
Pussy's Lesson	. . . .	*C. D. L.*	104
Quite a History. (After the German.)	. . . .	*Arlo Bates*	176
Race in the Air, A. Picture	. . . .		176
Rainy Day, A. Picture.	. . . .		88
Ready for her First Dip in the Big Ocean . . . } Picture, drawn by	. . . .	*C. M. Relyea*	144
Real Uncle Remus Story, A. Picture, drawn by .	. . .	*William E. Kline*	174
Robber Rat and the Poor Little Kitten, The	. . .	*Katharine Pyle*	99
Robin, The		*Anna Chase Davis*	100, 101
Santa Claus Street in Jingletown	. . . .	*Sarah J. Burke*	198
Scissors, The		*Laura E. Richards*	166
Second Kitten's Hunt, The		*Tudor Jenks*	160, 161
Shoe Play	. . . .	*Edith Godyear*	20
Shopping		*W. W. Gibson*	150
Sing, Sing! What Shall We Sing?			123
Something Between a Goose and a Peacock. Picture	. . . .		165
Song of the Skipping Rope, The		*Anna B. Patten*	130
"Speak!" Picture		*George Varian*	8
Story of the Morning-Glory Seed, The		*Margaret Eytinge*	178
Story of Mother Hubbard Told in Japanese Pictures, The	. . . .		169
Stranger Cat, The		*N. P. Babcock*	62, 63
Sunday, Sixpence in the Plate	. . . .	*William Wye Smith*	126
"Suppose!"		*E. L. Sylvester*	14
Taking Dolly's Photograph		*Sydney Dayre*	154
Tender-Hearted Arab, A		*Frederick B. Opper*	106
That Little Girl		*Claude Harris*	162
There's Nothing Very Important the Matter	. . . .		56
There Was a Small Servant Called Kate	. . . .		118
They Were Happy and did Laugh		*J. G. Francis*	122
Thimble, The		*Laura E. Richards*	168
"This Hat is Getting Too Small for Us." Picture, drawn by	*J. H. Dolph*		75
Thread, The		*Laura E. Richards*	167
Three Little Sisters. From a painting by William Page	. . . .		128
Tides, The		*Thomas Tapper*	157
Tilting		*A. De F. Lockwood*	95
Tired Little Mother, A		*Laura E. Richards*	32
Turkey's Nest, The		*Frank H. Sweet*	92
Up in a Balloon			181
"Upset Me if you Dare! Please Don't!" Picture	. . . .		125

		PAGE
Warrior Bold, A. Picture		92
Waterproof Folk	Agnes Lewis Mitchill	133
Way Things Vanish, The	Elizabeth Chase	170
Weather Receipt, A	Anna M. Pratt	143
Wee Little House with the Golden Thatch		126
What and Where?	Anna Hamilton	85
What Could the Farmer Do?	George William Ogden	138, 139, 140, 141
What Pussy Said	Sydney Dayre	14
"What Time Does Papa Come?" Picture		117
"When We Have Tea"	Thomas Tapper	31
Where's Mother?	Sarah S. Baker	51
Which of These Little Boys Lives in Your House? } Silhouette picture, drawn by Elise Böhm		24
Which of These Little Girls Lives in Your House? } Silhouette picture, drawn by Elise Böhm		25
Why Cherries Grow	Clinton Scollard	93
Windmill, The	M. M. D.	80, 81
Winter Day, A	M. L. Van Vorst	26
Wishes	Florence E. Pratt	152
Words Inclined to Jingle	Annie E. De Friese	119
Yankee Napoleon: "Bring on Your Duke of Wellington" } Picture		175

CHUMS.

Baby World.

THE BIG BOOBOO AND THE LITTLE BOOBOO.

BY GERTRUDE SMITH.

And one morning Robbie's father stood by his bed, and Robbie was sleeping, and sleeping, and sleeping.

"Boo—boo!" said Robbie's father.

Robbie opened his eyes and sat up.

"Boo—boo!" he answered sleepily.

"Boo—boo!" said his father again, and jumped at him.

"Boo—boo!" answered Robbie, and now his eyes were wide open.

Then the big Booboo took the little Booboo up in his arms and carried him down to the garden—for they lived all the time in the garden, and only slept in the house.

And the garden was full of roses, and daisies, and pinks, and many, many flowers besides.

In the shade of a great big tree was a tiny little lake. And what do you think? The little Booboo took off his nightgown and waded out into the lake!

He had his bath in the little lake in the garden — not in a bath-tub at all, but in the little lake in the garden.

The water came up, up, up to his chin, but he wasn't a bit afraid.

"I'm a fish! I'm a fish!" he shouted, and down he splashed and swam like a fish!

He was only four years old, the little Booboo, but he could certainly, certainly do a great many things for his age. He could swim as well as his father!

And the big Booboo sat on a rock and watched him.

He often swam in the lake himself, and knew what fun it was.

And little maid Annie came down the walk and told them that breakfast was ready.

So out of the water Robbie came, and soon had his legs in his trousers.

For the little Booboo wore trousers too, and a coat, and a pair of suspenders — just like his father's!

And then they went over to breakfast on the other side of the garden, — they always ate in the garden, — where mama came out and joined them.

But before they sat down to the table the big Booboo stood

on his head! on the smooth green lawn he stood on his head! It was a way he had, when he was glad, of surprising the little Booboo.

The table was set where the roses grew all over a shady arbor.

And little maid Annie brought out the cakes, and the toast, and the chocolate too.

Then mama, all dressed in blue and white, jumped out into sight from behind a bush, and said: "Boo—boo! Who knew?—not you. I have been all the time in the garden. I saw you taking your bath!"

And the big Booboo laughed, "Ha! ha!"

And the little Booboo laughed, "He! he! Did you see me?"

And so the day began—a happy, happy day.

For the big Booboo and the little Booboo always were thinking of things to do, and having the best of times.

NEW MOTHER GOOSE RHYMES.

Bow-wow, little dog, have you any name?
Yes sir, two, but they don't mean the same,
One from my master, he calls me "Champ",
And one from the neighbors, they call me "Scamp."

Finish your meal, then softly steal,
To see my fine lady try her new wheel.
She's bumps on both elbows,
A scratch on her nose;
But she doesn't care
If her wheel only goes.

Little Tom Barber
  Sat in the arbor
    Wearing a gay new tie.
Some other boys stared
As his graces he aired
Saying: "Don't we look fine!
    Oh my!"

Little Miss Crewe
  Has lost her shoe,
And can't tell where to find it.
Move out the chest,
And cease the quest,
For doggy
  and shoe
    are
      behind it.

BERTIE'S FIRST DAY AT SCHOOL.

[The following little story is told to a girl of three, by her mother. The mother imitates the voices of the different animals, and when she comes to the "A B C" part she takes an alphabet-card and the little girl shows her how Susie and Bertie said their letters to the teacher.]

ONE day Bertie's mama gave him a little book, and a tin pail full of nice things for dinner, and told him to go to school.

Bertie went a little way up the road, and met a dog. He began to be  lonely, for he had no one to walk with, so he said, "Doggie, don't you want to go to school with me?" But the dog said only, "Bow-wow!" and ran away.

Bertie went on, and pretty soon he met a lamb. "Don't you want to go to school with me?" said he.

But the lamb said only, "Bah! bah!" and ran away.

Then Bertie met a cow with long, sharp horns; but she did not look as if she would hurt a little boy. So he said, "Bossy, don't you want to go to school with me?" But the cow said only, "Moo-o, moo-o!" and went on eating grass.

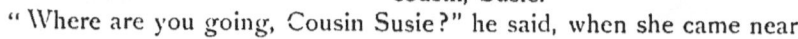

A little way on Bertie saw a pig. "Piggy, don't you want to go to school with me?" he said. But the pig only said, "Ugh! ugh!" and lay down in the sun.

By and by Bertie saw a path that came down a hill into the road. Just as he got to the path a little girl ran out into the road. It was Bertie's cousin, Susie.

"Where are you going, Cousin Susie?" he said, when she came near.

"I am going to school," said the little girl, showing him her books.

"Oh! there is where I am going," said Bertie. "May I go with you?"

"Yes," said Susie; "but we must hurry. Don't you hear the bell ringing? What have you in your pail?"

"A piece of bread and butter, a nice little pie, a nice little cake, and an apple," said Bertie.

By this time they were at the school, and they both went in.

The teacher asked their names.

Bertie told his name, and the little girl said her name was Susie.

Then they stood by the teacher and said—("What did they say?")—"A, B, C, D, E, F, G, H, I, J, K, L, M, N, O, P, Q, R, S, T, U, V, W, X, Y, Z."

When Bertie came home, he said: "Mama, I met a dog and asked him to go to school, and he said, 'Bow-wow!' and I asked a lamb and he said, 'Bah! bah!' and I asked a cow, and she said, 'Moo-o, moo-o!' and I asked a pig, and he said, 'Ugh! ugh!' and none of them would go with me. Then I met Cousin Susie, and *she* went with me."

MR. ELEPHANT RINGING THE BELL FOR DINNER.

H, the little man of Morrisburg
  Who would a-fishing go!
He put three fish into a tub,
  And thought he'd have a throw!
One was a dace, and one was a perch,
  And one was a speckled trout;
And just as sure as he put them in,
  He'd fail to pull them out!
Oh, the little man of Morrisburg,
  Who would a-fishing go!
With fisherman's rig, when he grows big
  He'll know just where to throw!

"SPEAK!"

THE DOLLS' CHRISTMAS DINNER.

MISS LILYWHITE'S PARTY.

"MAY I go to Miss Lilywhite's party?"
  But Grandmama shook her head:
  "When the birds go to rest,
    I think it is best
  For mine to go, too," she said.

"*Can't* I go to Miss Lilywhite's party?"
  Still Grandmama shook her head:
  "Dear child, tell me how.
    You're half asleep now;
  Don't ask such a thing," she said.

Then that little one's laughter grew hearty:
  "Why, Granny," she said,
  "Going to Miss Lilywhite's party
    Means going to bed!"

FERN-SEED.

If you gather all the fern-seed,—
  The little green fern-seed,—
And put it in your shoe, so they say,
  You can see a thousand things,
  You can fly, too, without wings,
And nobody can see you on your way.

So I hunted for the fern-seed,—
  The little green fern-seed,—
And I filled up all the space in my shoe;
  Then I hurried home to try
  If they 'd know that it was I,
And the first thing mother said was
      " Here is Lou ! "

DORA AND HER RING.

As little Dora was feeding some birds out of her window, a pretty ring slipped from her finger and fell, and nobody could find it. She felt very sorry, for the ring had been given to her by her grandmama. It was too large for her and she put it on only once in a while, and then would lay it away. Somebody said, " How foolish for her to feed the birds!" One day, three or four weeks after she lost the ring, Dora thought she would look for it again, and she found in the bushes beneath her window a bird's nest, and, peeping in, saw five little birds. The mother-bird flew around so wildly that Dora thought she would wait till some other day to look at the little baby-birds. But she got only a peep now and then, for the mother-bird kept watching as if she feared somebody would rob her nest. But one day in July, when all was still, Dora stood tip-toe and gazed into the nest. The birds had all gone, but she saw something shining brightly at the side of the nest where the birds had lived. It was her own precious ring, which had fallen into the nest! She never lost it again, and she was always glad that she fed the birds.

"DEAR ME, LUCY ANN, IF YOU'RE NOT MORE CAREFULLER OF YOURSELF, YOU…"

A FALL to the knees,   A spread of the hands,
  A turn of the toes,   And a dip of the nose.
    It takes all these just to say, "Good-day,"
     In the Japanese country, far away.

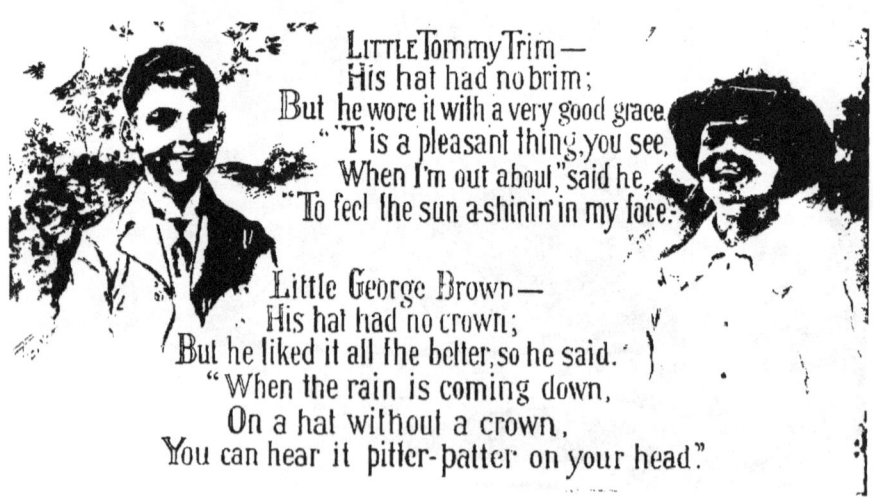

Little Tommy Trim—
His hat had no brim;
But he wore it with a very good grace.
"'T is a pleasant thing, you see,
When I'm out about," said he,
"To feel the sun a-shinin' in my face."

Little George Brown—
His hat had no crown;
But he liked it all the better, so he said.
"When the rain is coming down,
On a hat without a crown,
You can hear it pitter-patter on your head."

My tiny daughter Dolly
  Comes frowning from her walk.
"My hat 's so dreffle big," she says,
  "That I tan't see to talk!"

A POLITE OWL.

The owl made a bow
As I passed where she sat,—
A very small owl,—
She bowed this way and that,
So I lifted my hat.

Did she just bob her head
When the sun hurt her eyes?
So my grandfather said.
But she looked very wise
For an owl of her size.

BY SYDNEY DAYRE.

BESSIE with her kitten
    Sitting on her knee—
"Pussy, dear, now won't you
    Try to talk to me?
Yes, you pretty darling,
    I am sure you could
Say a little something
    If you only would.
Now, I'll ask a question.
    Answer, Pussy—*do!*
Whom do you love the very best?"
    And Pussy said: "M—you."

"SUPPOSE!"

SUPPOSE—sup-p-o-s-e—
Well, just suppose
Some day my mother'd say,
"You need n't go to school, my
    dear,
Just stay at home and play.
And here's a box of chocolate
    creams"
(Or something quite as good).
"Eat all you want!"—oh, just
    suppose,
Suppose my mother should!

"THE MOON MUST LOVE ME VERY MUCH, FOR, WHEN THE NIGHT IS FINE,
OF ALL THE WINDOWS IN THE WORLD, IT COMES AND SHINES THROUGH MINE!"

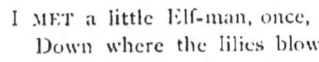

THE LITTLE ELF.

BY JOHN KENDRICK BANGS.

I MET a little Elf-man, once,
   Down where the lilies blow.
I asked him why he was so small
   And why he did n't grow.

He slightly frowned, and with his eye
   He looked me through and through.
"I 'm quite as big for me," said he,
   "As you are big for you."

The Conceited Mouse

By Ella Foster Case.

Once upon a time there was a very small mouse with a very, very large opinion of himself. What he did n't know his own grandmother could n't tell him.

"You 'd better keep a bright eye in your head, these days," said she, one chilly afternoon. "Your gran'ther has smelled a trap."

"Scat!" answered the small mouse; —"'s if I don't know a trap when I see it!" And that was all the thanks she got for her good advice.

"Go your own way, for you will go no other," the wise old mouse said to herself; and she scratched her nose slowly and sadly as she watched her grandson scamper up the cellar stairs.

"Ah!" sniffed he, poking his whiskers into a crack of the dining-room cupboard, "cheese—as I 'm alive!" Scuttle—scuttle. "I 'll be squizzled, if it is n't in that cunning little house; I know what that is—a cheese-house, of course. What a very snug hall! That's the way with cheese-houses. I know, 'cause I've heard the dairymaid talk about 'em. It must be rather inconvenient, though, to carry milk up that step and through an iron door. I know why it's so open — to let in fresh air. I tell you, that cheese is good! Kind of a reception-room in there — guess I know a reception-room from a hole in the wall. No trouble  at all about getting in, either. Wouldn't grandmother open her eyes to see me here! Guess I'll take another nibble at that cheese, and go out. What's that noise? What in squeaks is the matter with the door? This is a cheese-house, I know it is,—but what if it should turn out to be a — O-o-o-eeee!" And that's just what it did turn out to be.

End of ye Tale

THE Howlery Crowlery ROOM

By Laura E. Richards.

It does n't pay to be cross —
It's not worth while to try it;
For Mammy's eyes so sharp
Are very sure to spy it;

A pinch on Billy's arm,
A snarl or a sullen gloom,
No longer we stay, but must up and away
To the Howlery Growlery room.

Chorus. Hi! the Howlery! ho! the Growlery!
        Ha! the Sniffery, Snarlery, Scowlery!
        There we may stay,
        If we choose, all day;
        But it 's only a smile that can bring
            us away.

If Mammy catches me
A-pitching into Billy;
If Billy breaks my whip,
Or scares my rabbit silly:
It 's " Make it up, boys, quick!
Or else you know your doom!"
We must kiss and be friends, or the squabble ends
In the Howlery Growlery room.

Chorus. Hi! the Howlery! ho! the Growlery!
        Ha! the Sniffery, Snarlery, Scowlery!
        There we may stay,
        If we choose, all day;
        But it 's only a smile that can bring
            us away.

So it does n't pay to be bad;
There 's nothing to be won in it:
And when you come to think,
There 's really not much fun in it.
So, come! The sun is out,
The lilacs are all a-bloom.
Come out and play, and we 'll keep away
From the Howlery Growlery room.

Chorus. Hi! the Howlery! ho! the Growlery!
        Ha! the Sniffery, Snarlery, Scowlery!
        There we may stay,
        If we choose, all day;
        But it 's only a smile that can bring
            us away.

MUSIC FOR THE HOWLERY-GROWLERY ROOM.

SHOE PLAY.

BY EDITH GOODYEAR

Five frisky ponies waiting at the gate,
Shoe them, saddle them, and ride off in state.
One pony for my little man;
Two ponies make a span;
Three ponies in a row;
Four ponies ready to go;
Five ponies, glossy and bright
Up street, – down street,

And home again at night.

A little boy named Johnny
Had a donkey he called Ned,
Who when e'er he tried to ride him
Always threw him o'er his head.

AN IMAGINARY CASE.

If one little boy—being
Healthy and strong—
Can keep a house merry
All the day long,

Just think, if you can,
What a tempest of joys
There 'd be in a house
Holding nine little boys.

For a whole long week the little pet Pug was as good as he could be,
He did n't growl at the baby, nor spill his milk at tea;
And so, when the Circus came to town, they gave him a silver dime,
They put on his Sunday collar, and hoped he 'd have a good time.
He sat right next to the Lion (who had to have two seats),
And saw the clever animals perform their wonderful feats:
Two Poodles drew a Peacock in an elegant golden car,
While the Owl drove four sleek Rabbits—a livelier team by far;
Bruin balanced Reynard on a pole placed on his snout;
And the Hare danced a sailor's-hornpipe on a Pig that ran about;
Five Kittens rode in a basket on the back of a Dromedary;
While a Cat who walked on stilts was as graceful as a fairy;
A Rhinoceros played the organ—the tune was "Upidee."
But some of the jokes the Cat-clown made the pet Pug could n't see!

All this was in the nearest ring,—the other was lively, too:
To watch them both at once was all the little Pug could do,
While six performing Pussy cats were making a curious group.
At the very same time two Monkeys went diving through a hoop.
Two foreign birds were driven in harness by a Cat,
But a tiny Frog with a team of Chicks was a queerer sight than that!
Another Frog was a juggler and kept five balls in air,
Yet the Elephant balancing on a ball was the funniest creature there.
Above, near the top of the Circus tent, the Jocko Brothers bold
With their daring leaps from the high trapeze made the little Pug's blood
    run cold!
Near them hung a Cockatoo, who swung in a lofty ring,
And who did n't have a thing to do, but laugh at everything.
At last the band played "Home, Sweet Home," the animals all filed out,
And the little Pug went trotting away with plenty to talk about.

MORAL.

So, Pugs, don't growl at the baby, though the baby should pull your ears,
And maybe *you 'll* go to the Circus when it comes to your town, my
    dears!

"HE SAT RIGHT NEXT TO THE LION (WHO HAD TO HAVE TWO SEATS),
AND SAW THE CLEVER ANIMALS PERFORM THEIR WONDERFUL FEAT."
(SEE NEXT PAGE.)

WHICH of these little boys lives in your house?

Which of these little girls lives in your house?

A WINTER DAY.

Snow makes the fields and gardens white;
    It lies upon the roofs and ground.
It fell so softly in the night,
    When I was sleeping safe and sound.

I think I 'll go and get my sled,
    The little gloves my Grandma knit,
My cap with tabs, my jacket red —
    And try to coast a little bit.

"Go out before it melts away,"
    My mother said. I hope she 'll stand
There in the window, while I play,
    And smile and nod, and wave her hand.

"DON'T YOU THINK THAT WINTER'S PLEASANTER THAN ALL?"—

"BUT THEN, IN SUMMER, YOU CAN PLAY ON THE BEACH!"

THE FROG'S FOURTH OF JULY.

HAPPY little Frog! Of course he was going to see what Bobby, and Nelly, and Mamie, and Lee, and Louis, and Edith, and Philip intended to do. Afraid of fire-crackers?—who? *he?* No, indeed! So he did not heed his mother's warning, but hopped off to the lovely grove at Woodreve, the children's summer home.

The nurses Kate, and Annie, and Mary spread a nice luncheon of cake and lemonade on the grass under the trees. It was very warm, and the children played, and swung, and fired torpedoes, and set off fire-crackers. They were getting restless and tired, when Bobby said: "Let's fill a tomato-can with fire-crackers, turn it bottom up, tilt it a little, and set fire to one of the crackers with a match tied to a long pole." The plan was hailed with delight. So they fixed it all, and then sat down to enjoy the great fright of the nurses, who were sewing and knitting under a tree not very far from the can, but with their backs to it.

The little frog had been hiding in the grass near by, and he did not understand at all why everything was suddenly quiet — so he hopped, and he hopped, and he hopped, and at last he hopped up on the can, so that he might see better. There he sat, puffed out with pride and staring all about, while the children stared back at the foolish fellow,—when bang! bang! went the crackers,—up went the can,—and over went little Mr. Frog into a blackberry bush! The nurses screamed, the little girls shrieked, the lemonade was turned over, the cake upset, Edith's bottle of milk was broken, and such a time! But it did not last long, for fresh supplies came from the house. One of the ladies came out to ask what *was* the matter; and then all the children told the story, and laughed and laughed, at the fun. But the little frog rubbed his legs and scratched his head, wondering what had happened, and then hopped away to his home as fast as he could go — the most surprised little frog that ever saw a Fourth of July.

BANG! BANG!

The Grumpity Man

Highty, tighty, grumpity man!
Finding fault since your life began!
Pity we have n't a giant or two
To carry off grumpities such as you!

MY CHOICE.

By Delia Hart Stone.

If Maude were a little lady,
   Who did no work at all;
And if Kate were a little housemaid,
   Who did the work for all;

And if my little lady
   Were sad the livelong day;

And if the little housemaid
   Were always glad and gay:

I 'd rather be the housemaid,
   And do the work for all,
Than be the little lady,
   And never work at all.

By Thomas Tapper.

In winter-time, when we have tea,
We have to light the lamp to see;
The days are cold, the winds blow strong,
The sun's afraid to stay out long.

In summer-time, quite otherwise,
It seems he 's always in the skies;
The weather 's warm, he likes to stay,
And so we have our tea by day.

THE ELEPHANT AND THE GIRAFFE.

Said the elephant to the giraffe,
"Your neck is too long by one half."
He replied, "Since your nose
Reaches down to your toes
At others you 'd better not laugh."

A TIRED LITTLE MOTHER.

By Laura E. Richards.

When Nita heard her mother say, "I am really overworked, and all tired out!" she shook her curly head, and sighed, "Me, too, Mama!"

And no wonder! Her mother has only four children, while Nita has sixteen. She looks very young, does she not, to have such a large family? for this is Nita, in the picture. She says she has to work "all — day — long!" There are Nita's six grown-up children, and then come Medora, Selina Polly, Mungo Park (Papa named him), and the twins, Pinky and Winky, and Shadrach, Meshach, and Abednego. (The last three are black, and no one could tell one from the other, but it does n't matter.)

Then there are Seraphina, and Jim and Jam, another pair of twins, and Mr. and Mrs. Wobblechin, and the Red Rover, and Bridget, the cook doll, and Gwen, the Welsh dairywoman. There is the baby, too, — I forgot her, — and that makes seventeen. And all these dolls have to be fed and clothed, and put to bed, and taken up again. They are always put to bed; but sometimes they don't get taken up for a good while but then — one can always play they're sick, so that does n't count. Jim and Jam have had the fever ten times, and once Jim had it so badly that his legs came off. Yes, that was something like a fever. Papa is a doctor, and he said he never had such a case as that in all his days.

Now, when this picture was taken, Nita had just been having a dreadful time with Selina Polly. Selina had the "ammonia in the back of her head," — Mama thought it was a crack, caused by dropping her on the hearth, but Nita said it was ammonia, and of course it must have been; and her neck began to "get all wobbly," Nita said, and it was perfectly dreadful. Nita had n't had a wink of sleep for three whole nights, and she had n't tasted a morsel of food; for how could she eat when her child was in that state, with her strength all wasting away, hour after hour. So, at last, after walking up and down the nursery for about a week, or it might be a fortnight, Nita just lay down for a minute on the cushion, one afternoon before she was made ready for tea, because she thought the change might be good for Selina Polly. It was a very hot day, but Nita was not sleepy — "not one single tiny bit of a scrap!" she told nurse. So, then — nothing happened for a good while, and *then* nurse said it was tea-time, and told Nita that she had had a good nap.

This shows how foolish even the best of nurses sometimes are; for how *could* she *really* suppose that a mother would take naps, when her child's head was in danger of falling off?

A TIRED LITTLE MOTHER.

HERE ARE TWENTY-SIX GOOD FRIENDS OF EVERY LITTLE GIRL AND BOY.
WHO CAN NAME THEM ALL?

THAT'S THE WAY!

By Ella Wheeler Wilcox.

Just a little every day,
      That's the way
Seeds in darkness swell and grow,
Tiny blades push through the snow.
Never any flower of May
Leaps to blossom in a burst.
Slowly — slowly — at the first.
      That's the way!
Just a little every day.

Just a little every day,
      That's the way
Children learn to read and write,
Bit by bit, and mite by mite.
Never any one, I say,
Leaps to knowledge and its power.
Slowly — slowly — hour by hour.
      That's the way!
Just a little every day.

A MAY-DAY PARTY IN CENTRAL PARK.

THE RHYME OF TEN LITTLE RABBITS

BY KATE N. MYTINGER

1 little rabbit, <u>one</u>
went out in the
field to run.

2 little rabbits, <u>two</u>
Said they didn't
know what to do.

3 little rabbits, <u>three</u>
Said: "Let us
climb a tree."

4 little rabbits, <u>four</u>
Said: "Let's swing
on the old barn door."

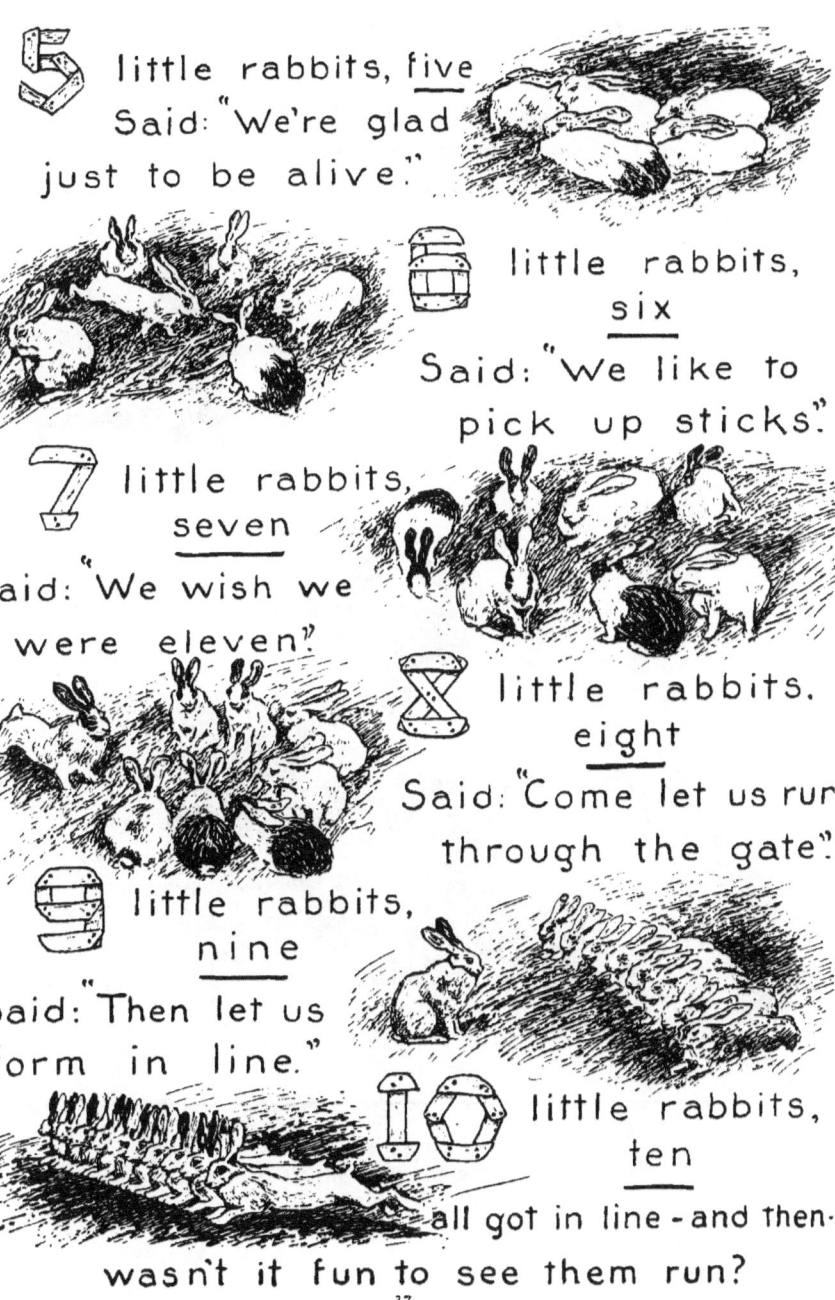

5 little rabbits, five
Said: "We're glad just to be alive."

6 little rabbits, six
Said: "We like to pick up sticks."

7 little rabbits, seven
Said: "We wish we were eleven."

8 little rabbits, eight
Said: "Come let us run through the gate."

9 little rabbits, nine
Said: "Then let us form in line."

10 little rabbits, ten all got in line – and then wasn't it fun to see them run?

THREE KINDS OF SEE-SAW.

See-saw I saw in the fields one day;
A see-saw you'll see when the children play;--
And oh! the very funniest way

IN THE FIELD.

To see a see-saw, I know you'll say,
Is when at the biggest show in town,
The elephants see-saw, up and down:

MARY ANN: "EDDY WHITE, IF YOU DARE TO JUMP OFF, I'LL NEVER SPEAK TO YOU AGAIN, THE LONGEST DAY THAT I LIVE! NEVER!"

TRAINED BABY ELEPHANTS PLAYING SEE-SAW

THE FATE OF A GINGER-BREAD MAN.

Here's a nice brown ginger-bread man,
Freshly baked in the baker's pan,
Spiced and sugared, and spick and span;
Cloves for his eyes and paste for his tie—
Oh, what a nice sweet man to buy!

Here are Felix and Mary Ann
Looking in at the ginger-bread man
(Spiced and sugared, and spick and span,
Cloves for his eyes and paste for his tie),
Wondering whether the price is high.

Here are Felix and Mary Ann
Going home with the ginger-bread man
That was baked in the baker's pan.
"Far too nice to be eaten," they said;
"Keep the man for a dolly, instead."

Here behold the ginger-bread man,
That was baked in the baker's pan,
In the doll-house of Mary Ann.
See him stand, with his round, fat face,
Among the dolls in silk and lace!

Here are Felix and Mary Ann
Sleeping sound as ever they can,
Dreaming about the ginger-bread man
Left in the doll-house, set away,
Till they wake in the morn to play.

See this rat; since the night began
He has prowled to get what he can.
Ah, he smells the ginger-bread man!
There's the doll-house under the shelf,
Just where the rat can climb himself!

Every rat will get what he can.
Ah, the poor, sweet ginger-bread man!
Wake, O Felix and Mary Ann!
There's a patter, a jump, a squeak—
Ah, if the ginger-bread man could speak!

See the rat, as quick as he can,
Climbing up for the ginger-bread man
In the doll-house of Mary Ann!
Ah, if the ginger-bread man could run!
Oh, to see what the rat has done!

Here are Felix and Mary Ann
Come to play with the ginger-bread man,
Spiced and sugared, and spick and span.
Ah, behold where he stood before,
Only crumbs on the doll-house floor!

I've grown so big, I go to school,
  And write upon a slate,
And say now, two and two make four,
  And four and four make eight.
  And eight less four is four, you know,
  And four less eight is—wait!—
  I'll put it down—
    Oh dear,
      oh, dear!
        Now
        what *is*
        four less eight?

NAMING DOLLY.

My darling Dolly is one week old; —
   Her forehead is fair and creamy,
Her cheeks are pink and her hair is gold,
   And her eyes are dark and dreamy.
She 's lovely and sweet as she can be;
   She 's Santa Claus' own little daughter,
But she came to me on the Christmas Tree: —
   How glad I am that he brought her!

I never am lonely since she came,
   And the only trouble with me is
That I have n't been able to find a name
   One half as pretty as she is.
Mama 's in favor of "Isabel";
   And papa says "Betsy or Polly!"
And I 've thought and thought and maybe — well,
   I think I shall call her Dolly.

GOING VISITING WITH DOLLY.

I KEEP my Dolly so warm and nice
   This cloudy, stormy weather.
My Dolly and I are quiet as mice
   Whenever we play together.
And yet we have the pleasantest play —
   Would you like to ask "What is it?"
Why, over and over, every day,
   My Dolly and I "go visit."

Sometimes on "Towser" we like to call,
   Or travel to see the Kitty;
'T is Grandpa's farm just out in the hall,
   And the parlor is Boston City;
'T is mama's house in the corner there,
   And then, when the lamps are lighted,
My papa's at home in his easy-chair,
   And Dolly and I are invited.

"FIDDLE-DIDDLE-DEE!"

LITTLE DAVIE ran through the garden,—a great slice of bread and butter in one hand, and his spelling-book in the other. He was going to study his lesson for to-morrow.

You could not imagine a prettier spot than Davie's "study," as he called it. It was under a great oak-tree, that stood at the edge of a small wood. The little boy sat down on one of the roots and opened his book.

THIS IS THE LITTLE WREN.

"But first," thought he, "I'll finish my bread and butter."

So he let his book drop, and, as he ate, he began to sing a little song with which his mother sometimes put the baby to sleep. This is the way the song began:

> "I bought a bird, and my bird pleased me;
> I tied my bird behind a tree;
> Bird said ——"

"Fiddle-diddle-dee!" sang something, or somebody, behind the oak. Davie looked a little frightened, for that was just what he was about to sing in his song. But he jumped up and ran around to the other side of the tree. And there was a little brown wren, and it had a little golden thread around its neck, and the thread was tied to a root of the big tree.

"Hello!" said Davie, "was that you?"

Now, of course Davie had not expected the wren to answer him. But the bird turned her head on one side, and, looking up at Davie, said:

"Yes, of course it was! Who else did you suppose it could be?"

"Oh yes!" said Davie, very much astonished. "Oh yes, of course! But I thought you only did it in the song!"

"Well," said the wren, "were not you singing the song, and am not I in the song, and what else could I do?"

"Yes, I suppose so," said Davie.

"Well, go on, then," said the wren, "and don't bother me."

Davie felt very queer. He stopped a moment, but soon thought that

THIS IS THE GUINEA-HEN.

he must do as he was bid, and he began to sing again:

> "I bought a hen, and my hen pleased me;
> I tied my hen behind a tree;
> Hen said ——"

"Shinny-shack! shinny-shack!" interrupted another voice, so loudly that Davie's heart gave a great thump, as he turned around. There, behind the wren, stood a little Bantam hen, and around her neck was a little golden cord that fastened her to the wren's leg.

"I suppose that was you?" said Davie.

"Yes, indeed," replied the hen. "I know when my time comes in, in a song. But it was provoking for you to call me away from my chicks."

"I?" cried Davie. "I did n't call you!"

"Oh, indeed!" said the Bantam. "It was n't you, then, who were singing 'Tied my hen,' just now! Oh no, not you!"

"I 'm sorry," said Davie. "I did n't mean to."

"Well, go on, then," said the little hen, "and don't bother."

Davie was so full of wonder that he did not know what to think of it all. He went back to his seat, and sang again:

> "I had a guinea, and my guinea pleased me;
> I tied my guinea behind a tree ——"

But here he stopped, with his mouth wide open; for up a tiny brown path that led into the wood, came a little red man about a foot high, dressed in green, and leading by a long yellow string a plump, speckled guinea-hen! The little old man came whistling along until he reached the Bantam, when he fastened the yellow string to her leg, and went back again down the path, and disappeared among the trees.

THIS IS THE DUCK.

Davie looked and wondered. Presently, the guinea stretched out her neck and called to him in a funny voice:

"Why in the world don't you go on? Do you think I want to wait all day for my turn to come?"

Davie began to sing again: "Guinea said ——"

"Pot-rack! pot-rack!" instantly squeaked the speckled guinea-hen.

Davie jumped up. He was fairly frightened now. But his courage soon came back. "I'm not afraid," he said to himself; "I'll see what the end of this song will be!"—and he began to sing again:

"I bought a duck, and my duck pleased me;
I tied my duck behind a tree;
Duck said —— "

"Quack! quack!" came from around the oak. But Davie went on:

"I bought a dog, and the dog pleased me;
I tied my dog behind a tree;
Dog said —— "

"Bow-wow!" said a little curly dog, as Davie came around the spreading roots of the tree. There stood a little short-legged duck tied to the guinea's leg, and to the duck's leg was fastened the wisest-looking Scotch terrier, with spectacles on his nose and a walking-cane in his paw.

The whole group looked up at Davie, who now felt perfectly confident. He sat down on a stone close by, and continued his song:

"I had a horse, and my horse pleased me;
I tied my horse behind a tree."

Davie stopped and looked down the little brown path. Then he clapped his hands in great delight; for there came the little old man leading by a golden bridle a snow-white pony, no bigger than Davie's Newfoundland dog.

"Sure enough, it is a boy!" said the pony, as the old man tied his bridle to the dog's hind leg, and then hurried away. "I thought so! Boys are always bothering people."

"Who are you, and where did you all come from?" asked delighted Davie.

"Why," said the pony, "we belong to the court of Her Majesty the Queen of the Fairies. But, of course, when the song in which any of the court voices are wanted, is sung, they all have to go."

"I'm sure I'm very sorry," said Davie. "But why have n't I ever seen you all before?"

"Because," said the pony, "you have never sung the song down here before." And then he added: "Don't you think, now that we are all here, you'd better sing the song right end first, and be done with it?"

"Oh, certainly!" cried Davie, "certainly!" beginning to sing.

If you could but have heard that song! As Davie sang, each fowl or animal took up its part, and sang it, with its own peculiar tone and manner, until they all joined in.

> "I had a horse, and my horse pleased me;
> I tied my horse behind a tree.
> Horse said, 'Neigh! neigh!'
> Dog said, 'Bow-wow!'
> Duck said, 'Quack! quack!'
> Guinea said, 'Pot-rack! pot-rack!'
> Hen said, 'Shinny-shack! shinny-shack!'
> Bird said, 'Fiddle-diddle-dee!'"

Davie was overjoyed. He thought he would sing it all over again. But just then he was sure that his mother called him.

"Wait a minute!" he said to his companions. "Wait a minute! I'm coming back! Oh, it's just like a fairy-tale!" he cried to himself, as he bounded up the garden-walk. "I wonder what mother'll think?"

But his mother said she had not called him, and so he ran back as fast as his legs would carry him.

But they were all gone. His speller lay on the ground, open at the page of his lesson; a crumb or two of bread was scattered about; but not a sign of the white pony and the rest of the singers.

"Well," said Davie, as he picked up his book, "I guess I won't sing it again, for I bothered them so. But I wish they had stayed a little longer."

A BOOK-LOVER.

"I DO love books!" said Marjorie,
  One morning as she played.
And so she did, as you can see—
  This clever little maid!

The dictionary was her chair;
  The atlas big, her table;
The dolls sat up on other books
  As straight as they were able.

And then they all partook of tea,
  And did as they were bid.
"I do love books!" said Marjorie.
  Now, don't you think she did?

Moonlight, starlight —
  How many lights there be!
Little swinging lanterns
  On the ships at sea.
Green lights, yellow lights,
  Crimson lights aglow —
I see them shine on winter nights
  In mist and snow.

Big boats, little boats —
  How many boats there be!
Little swinging life-boats
  On the ships at sea.
I go on the ferry-boat,
  Mother goes with me;
I wish some day that we would float
  Far out to sea!

A FAMILY GROUP. OUR BOY, OUR GIRL, OUR BABY, AND OUR CAT.

CAMPING.

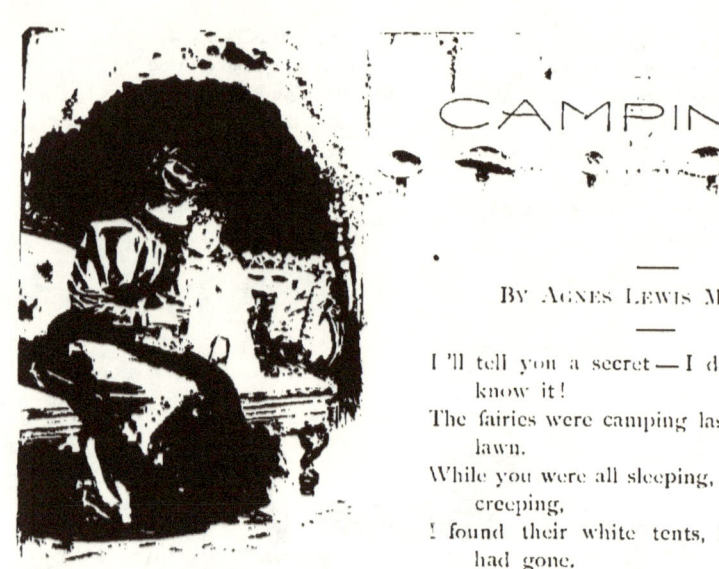

By Agnes Lewis Mitchill.

I'll tell you a secret — I don't think you know it!
The fairies were camping last night on the lawn.
While you were all sleeping, outdoors softly creeping,
I found their white tents, but the fairies had gone.

They were in a great flurry, or why should they hurry?
To leave their white tents was a queer thing to do.
Perhaps they come only at night, when 't is lonely.
I guess they are sly gipsy fairies — Don't you?

WHERE'S MOTHER?

Bright curly heads pop in all day
 To ask, "Is Mother here?"
Then give an eager glance
 around,
 And swiftly disappear.

She ought to wear a silver bell,
 Whose note, so sweet and
 clear,
Should tinkle out a cheery
 sound,
 Repeating, "Mother's near."

And then, if any little one
 Had something glad to tell,
Or scratches, bumps, or tears,
 or *tears*,
 Or secret woes befell.

No need to fly from room to room,
 But simply listen well,
And, like the happy little lambs,
 Just follow "Mother's" bell.

Sarah S. Baker.

PUSSY AND HER ELEPHANT.

By Hannah More Johnson.

Have you heard of little Pussy, in that country o'er the sea,
How the dogs came out to chase her and she had to climb a tree?
You have n't? Then I 'll tell you how gentle Pussy Gray
Went climbing up, hand over hand, and safely got away.

But then the strangest trouble came! The tree began to shake!
A tremendous giant something took Pussy by the neck
And tossed her off! And there again among the dogs was she,
And what could frightened Pussy do, but climb the same old tree?

But then the strange thing came again, and, swinging high in air,
Pounced right on little Pussy, as she sat trembling there;
But when it touched her fur it stopped; as though its owner thought:
"It's nothing but a pussy-cat that trouble here has brought.

"I'll let her make herself at home."—
And Pussy, safe once more,
Folded her paws contentedly and
  viewed the country o'er,
And purred a meek apology: "Excuse
  me, friend, I see
I've climbed a broad-backed elephant;
  I meant to climb a tree!"

Whatever else she said or sung that
  you would like to hear
She must have whispered coaxingly
  into the giant ear;
For often afterward, 't is said, Miss Pussy Gray was seen
To ride the broad-backed elephant as proud as any queen!

"A LION MET A LITTLE BOY
WELL VERSED IN HUNTER'S LORE;
THEN SPAKE HE TO THAT WELL READ BOY:
'WOULDST LIKE TO HEAR ME ROAR?'"

"'YES, THANK YOU,' SAID THE LITTLE BOY,
WHO SCORNED ALL PALTRY FRIGHT;
THE LION ROARED; THEN ASKED THE BOY:
'WOULDST LIKE TO SEE ME BITE?'"

"Oh yes", replied that plucky boy,
  Who coolly eyed his gun;
"But first I'd like to try this toy;—
  Wouldst like to see some fun?"

Then fled that lion from the boy,
  As beast ne'er ran before;—
And to this day that little boy
  Enjoys his hunter's lore.

1 WAS a wide-awake little boy
Who rose at the break of day;

2 were the minutes he took to dress,
Then he was off and away.

3 were his leaps when he cleared the stairs,
Although they were steep and high;

4 was the number which caused his haste,
Because it was Fourth of July!

5 were the pennies which went to buy
A package of crackers red;

6 were the matches which touched them off,
And then — he was back in bed.

7 big plasters he had to wear
To cure his burns so sore;

8 were the visits the doctor made
Before he was whole once more.

9 were the tiresome days he spent
In sorrow and pain; but then,

0 are the seconds he'll stop to **think**
Before he does it again.

THERE'S NOTHING VERY IMPORTANT THE MATTER,—
I'M ONLY THE ONLY SON OF A HATTER.

PHŒBE brings the tea-pot, the tea is all a-steam;
Dolly brings the pitcher filled with golden cream.
Rhoda has the dainty cups rimmed about with blue,
And Polly brings the pretty spoons shining bright as new.
The Baby trips along behind, looking very droll;
And she, the sweetest of them all, brings the sugar-bowl.

A PROBLEM IN THREES.

If three little houses stood in a
    row,
  With never a fence to divide,
And if each little house had three
    little maids
  At play in the garden wide,
And if each little maid had three little
    cats
  (Three times three times three),
And if each little cat had three little
    kits,
  How many kits would there be?

And if each little maid had three
    little friends
  With whom she loved to play,
And if each little friend had three
    little dolls
  In dresses and ribbons gay,
And if friends and dolls and cats
    and kits
  Were all invited to tea,
And if none of them all should send
    regrets,
  How many guests would there be?

Bingo, Buster and Beau

By James Harvey Smith.

Bingo is thirty inches high,
   And Buster thirty-two;
While Beau, who is n't quite so big,
   Is their loving friend and true.

Beau, the children's joy and pride,
   Is a black Newfoundland dog,
Bingo and Buster ponies are
   From the land of rain and fog.

No whip nor spur the little chaps
   Need when the children ride;
They prance and caper on the road,
   While Beau runs by their side.

Two little steeds and one big dog
   Make a fine sight to see;
Two little girls in a yellow cart —
   And they all belong to me!

I think nobody has more fun
   Or makes a braver show,
Than the little girls who ride behind
   Bingo, Buster, and Beau.

HOW CURIOUS!

By Tudor Jenks.

Said one little girl to another little girl
   As proudly as could be,
"I'll tell you something very nice
   That my papa told me:
He said I was the sweetest girl
   That ever there could be!"

Said the other little girl to that one little girl
   "Why, now!—how can you be?
For that is just the very same thing
   That my papa told me!"
(And neither was as sweet as *my* little girl—
   As any one could see!)

"ANA MANA MONA MIKE"

By Lee Carter.

In the empty room we three
   Play the games we always like,
And count to see who "it" shall be —
   Ana, mana, mona, mike.

Round and round the rhyme will go
   Ere the final word shall strike,
Counting fast or counting slow —
   Barcelona, bona, strike.

What it all means no one knows.
   Mixed up like a peddler's pack,
As from door to door he goes —
   Hare, ware, frow, frack.

Now we guess and now we doubt,
   Words enough or words we lack,
Till the rhyming brings about
   Welcomed with a farewell shout —
Hallico, ballico, wo-wi-wo-wack, You are OUT!

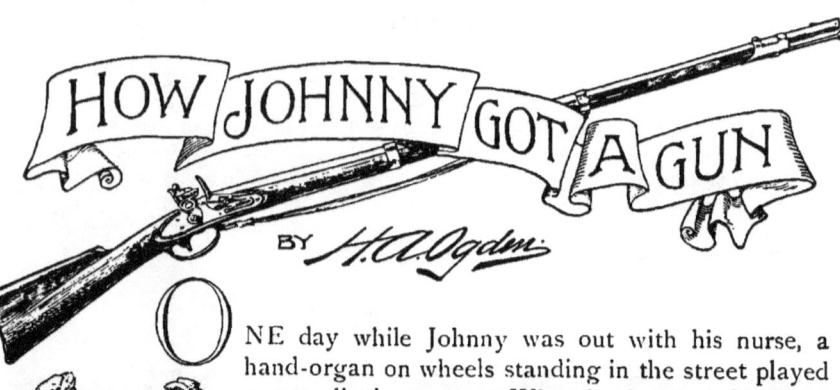

HOW JOHNNY GOT A GUN

BY H. A. Ogden

ONE day while Johnny was out with his nurse, a hand-organ on wheels standing in the street played a very lively tune. "What is that tune?" asked Johnny. "I like it." So the nurse asked the organ-grinder. "That-a tune-a he call 'Johnny, get your gun,'" said the man.

Johnny kept thinking "what a funny name for a tune!" And the next day he went into the room where his papa was painting a picture. After a while papa left Johnny by himself, and—what do you suppose happened? Everything was still, and Johnny was wondering what he'd do next, when in through the open window came the sound of a street-boy singing at the top of his voice.

Johnny knew the song at once. It was "Johnny, get your gun, get your gun, get your gun," and our Johnny thought to himself, "I'd like to get a gun. Where can I find one?"

Looking about, Johnny saw, standing against the wall on one side of the room, seven guns — some very big and some not so big. They belonged to his papa, and he used them when he painted pictures of soldiers.

Johnny trotted over and picked out (as a *little* boy always does) the biggest he could find. It happened to be an old gun, one of the kind that were used long ago, with a rusty lock and barrel.

None of the guns were loaded, so Johnny was in no danger; but he never thought of danger. Down from its place he lifted the gun and put it on the floor, and pulled away at the ramrod, and at last got it out. Then he tried to put it back in its place, but it went into the barrel instead. Then he tried the lock; but try as he might, it would n't work. "How do they shoot it?" he wondered.

"This way, I guess," said he; but he could not lift the big gun up to his shoulder.

Just then the curtains of the door opened, and there stood his papa!

"Why, my boy, what *are* you doing?" he asked. "You might drop that big gun on your toes. Why *did* you get that gun?"

"Why, papa, I heard somebody outside singing 'Johnny, get your gun,' and I did n't have any; so I thought I'd get one of yours. This was the biggest I could find."

His father put the gun back in its place, and told Johnny that he should have a gun of his very own if he would promise not to touch the big ones again.

Johnny promised. So a new gun was bought for him, a toy-gun that just fitted his little hands; and now when Johnny hears the song, he says, "*I'm* a Johnny, and I have a gun. I'll go and get it!"

The Stranger Cat.

A little girl with golden hair
Was rocking in her grand-ma's chair,
When in there walked a Stranger Cat—
(I'm sure there's nothing strange in that.)

It was a Cat with kinky ears
And very aged for it's years.
The little girl remarked "O Scat!"
(I <u>think</u> there's nothing strange in that)

But presently with stealthy tread
The cat, which at her word had fled,
Returned with cane, and boots and hat—
(I <u>fear</u> there's something strange in that.)

"Excuse me," and the cat bowed low,
"I hate to trouble you, you know,
But tell me, have you seen a rat?"
(I <u>know</u> there's something strange in that)

The little girl was very shy—
"Well really I can't say that I
Have seen one lately, Mr Cat."
(I'm <u>sure</u> there's something strange in that)

"O haven't you?" the Cat replied;
"Thanks, I am deeply gratified.
I really couldn't eat a rat."
(We <u>all</u> know what to think of that.)

And then the Cat with kinky ears
And so much wisdom for its years
Retired, with a soft pit-a-pat
(And that was all there was of that)

· N. P. Babcock.

HO, FOR THE CHRISTMAS-TREE!

THE BROTHERS.

By Agnes Lewis Mitchill.

I.

One little brother is short and slow;
The other is taller, and he can run,
For he takes twelve steps with his longer leg
While his brother is taking one.

II.

One little brother a bell must ring,
With every step that he slowly makes.
But the other runs gaily from morn till night
Nor cares to notice the steps he takes.

He who loves riddles may guess me this one,—
Who are the brothers and where do they run?

THE CLOSE OF THE DAY.

By M. L. V.

What is it comes at the close of the day,
　When the old world's tired and slowly swings?
Supper-time, bed-time, and nurse to say
　"Put up the toys and the play-house things!"
And we watch the shadows that glide and fall
On the shining floor and the nursery wall.

But that is n't all! Then we creep upstairs
　And soon begins a great pillow-fight,
As we chase one another over the chairs.
　Then we jump into bed, and we say "Good-night!"
And the tired old world more slowly swings,
And Mother sits in the dark and sings.

FROM "FIDO."

A LETTER FROM A PET DOG.

SEE HERE! I am a pet dog. My name is Fido. I belong to a little girl whose name is Sally. She has always been very good to me, and I never snap nor growl at her, for I do not need to. But I have some young puppies to bring up, and do not like the way she treats them. I am too shy to speak to her about this; but, as she reads Baby World, I have made up my mind to write you a letter so that you can print it. Then she will read it, and it will make her stop doing the things I do not like.

While puppies are small it is good for them to sleep nearly all the time. Now, as soon as I have put mine to sleep, Sally is sure to come and take one of them to play with. What would she think if I went up to the nursery and took her baby sister out of the cradle to play with?

One day she took "White Nose," my smallest puppy, and carried him into the hall. Here she sat down in grandpa's big chair, took a lump of sugar from the bowl, and tried to make White Nose eat it! Was n't she silly? It made my mouth water to see her waste good sugar on a puppy that had no teeth. I tried to show her that it was better for me to eat sugar than to let White Nose have it. I even sat up and begged for it. White Nose only kicked at it with his fat little legs, and was afraid the sugar would bite him.

I hope Sally, after she reads my letter, will see that it is best to give sugar to big dogs, and to let little puppies sleep until they have some teeth.

Your friend,   FIDO.

"SHE TRIED TO MAKE WHITE NOSE EAT THE SUGAR"

"I say good night and go up-stairs,
And then undress and say my prayers
Beside my bed, and then jump in it,
And then—the very nextest minute,
The morning sun comes in to peep
At me. I s'pose I 've been to sleep.
But seems to me," said little Ted,
"It 's not worth while to go to bed."

THE KETTLE.
BY LAURA E. RICHARDS.

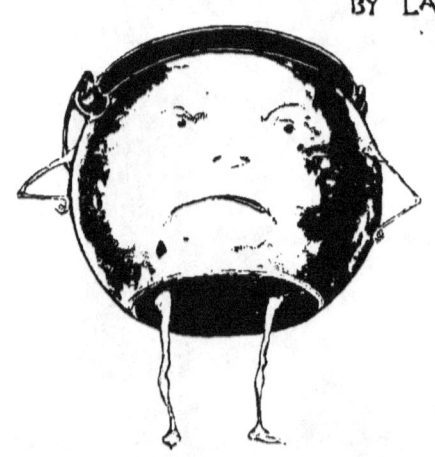

Oh, I am a kettle! a kettle am I!
  I never shall strive to deny it.
There 's nothing about me that 's sneaking or sly.
  Whatever I say, I stand by it.
Bubble, I say! and hubble, I say!
Some folks may not like it, but that is my way.
I mind my own business, and give no trouble;
Bubble, hub-bubble, hub-bubble, hub-bubble!

They say I am black; I admit it is true:
  A good, honest tint, and I love it.
I never, no, never set out to be blue;
  As for yellow or red, I 'm above it.
Bubble, I say, and hubble, I say!
I 'm ready to talk any time of the day.
Heap on the coals, and my song I will double;
Bub-bub-bub-bubble, bub-bubble, bub-bubble!

A QUEER little man kept an alphabet
    shop,
And out from his counter, hippity hop,
He danced until he was ready to drop,
Singing and shouting with never a stop:
    "Come in, little scholars,
    With bright silver dollars,
    Or if you've not any
    Then come with a penny.
        I have bumble Bs
        And marrowfat Ps,
        Some Chinese Qs

And Japanese Ts,
A flock of Js
And lots of Es,
And perfectly beautiful dark-blue Cs.
This is the place to buy your
    knowledge
At cheaper rates than are given at
    college!"
Then he'd draw a long breath and spin
    like a top,
This queer little man in an alphabet
    shop.

LITTLE MISCHIEF.

ONCE there was a little boy named Leslie. He lived in New York, quite near the Central Park. He would have been a good boy if he had not been so full of mischief. One day at the breakfast table, he upset his bowl of milk to make his papa laugh. And when his papa did not laugh, Leslie

began to cry. Then he was very sorry for doing such mischief. He did not have any more milk for that breakfast, and he thought he never would upset his bowl again. On the next day his nurse was going to the Central Park with him and a little boy named Vic, who was coming to spend the afternoon with him, so Leslie soon became very happy, and he talked a good deal about the Park, and all he was going to show Vic there.

"I'll show him the ammamuls," said Leslie (for he had not yet learned to say animals plainly), "and the Olbisct — that great high stone thing with writin' on it; and I'm goin' to take him to see the sheep and the lambs all jumpin' and playin' like everything. Can't I, Mamma?"

"Oh, yes," said his mamma; "but that high stone thing in the Park is an Obelisk. Can't you say Obelisk?"

"Olbisct," said Leslie, with such a funny twinkle in his bright eyes that his mamma thought he could say it better if he tried very hard.

Well, at last, it was nearly time for Vic to come. Nurse washed Leslie's face and dressed him finely to go to the Park. Then she told him he could go down-stairs and wait till she was ready. Leslie went straight to papa's room, but papa had gone up the street. So the little boy threw his pretty velvet hat on the table, and looked about for something to do.

And now something very bad happened. A pair of scissors lay on papa's table, and Leslie was up to mischief at once. He took the scissors and sat down on a bench close to some books and pictures that were lying on a big chair — and oh! what do you think he did? It was dreadful.

He cut two pages of one of the books; and he pulled the pictures to the floor. Then he began to cut one of the fine pictures!

Just then papa came in. He shouted to Leslie to stop, and then he said he must punish his little boy for such mischief.

Leslie cried very hard, for he knew he had done wrong, but as soon as he heard the door-bell ring, he stopped crying, and said:

"Oh, Papa! there's Vic! I must go now. We are going with nursey to see the ammamuls and lambs in the Park! I'll let you punish me a little when we get back."

But his papa said: "No, sir, you can not go to the Park to-day. You must GO RIGHT TO BED."

Leslie cried and cried and cried, but he had to go.

Papa felt very sad, but he told Victor that Leslie could not go out at all. Then he took Victor to the Park, himself, and showed him the Obelisk and the lambs, and the seals, and a good many things besides.

That same evening papa carried up Leslie's supper, and talked with him a while. He told the little boy what harm he had done, and how very naughty it was to injure books or pictures or anything of value, and how he hoped that after this he always could trust his little son. Then Leslie kissed him, and promised never, never to do such mischief again.

• A •
• family •
• Drive •

Old Bob, young Bob,
Little Bob and big
Molly Bob and Polly Bob
And Polly Bobby's pig,
All went for a drive one day
And strange as it may seem
They drove six miles and back again
And never hurt the team •

THE BOY AND THE TOOT.

By M. S.

There was a small boy, with a toot,
Whom the neighbors all threatened to shoot;
But the toot the next day,
Was filled full of clay,
Which stopped all the toot of the toot

BOB'S WAY.

By Tudor Jenks.

St. Nicholas belongs to Bob,
   Because our Uncle Jim
When he subscribed, last Christmas Day,
   Had it addressed to him.

But when it comes, why, I can't wait —
   To read it — till Bob 's through;
And Bob, who 's always good to me,
   Found out a way to do.

So, while he 's reading on one page,
   I 'm reading on another.
It 's just like Bob. — Whatever 's his
   He shares it with his brother.

"THIS HAT IS GETTING TOO SMALL FOR US."

GOOD FRIENDS.

Tabby was a great traveler. She knew every spot about the house—from attic to cellar—and just where everything that she liked was kept. There was hardly a rat or a mouse on the place that could hide from her. She crawled into every dark corner of the barn; could tell the number of eggs in each hen's nest; and often she took long walks through the fields, creeping through every hole in the fence that was as big as her body.

Besides all this, she rode about the farm-yard a great many times. She had merry rides with little Harry in his baby-carriage, with Johnny and Fred as horses; she had lain curled up on the great load of hay when Mr. Dorr and the men drove in from the fields; and she had traveled ever so many miles in the empty wagon, when the boys played it was a train of cars. She liked this railroad journey best; but Fred always waked her up at every station by his loud Too—oo—oo—t! At other times, she did not know that they were moving, even when Fred said they were dashing along at a terrible rate!

But such a ride as the one I shall tell about, she never had had before in all her life! Indeed, she would never have taken it—but she could not help it. Ponto made her go. You see, Ponto and Tabby were good friends. They lived and ate together; they ran races and played all sorts of nice games; and they liked each other very much. Sometimes they had little quarrels; but they soon forgot their anger and were friends again.

Every evening, when Ponto came into the yard, the two friends would run down one little hill from the house and up another little hill to the barn where Mary was milking. Ponto would keep the pigs out of the yard, and Tabby would watch every hole in the barn floor for a rat or a mouse. Then, when Mary was done milking, she would pour some fresh milk into a pan for Tabby to drink.

But, after a while, there came a long rain-storm. Ponto had to stay in the yard for two or three days. Tabby did nothing but doze! It seemed as if it never would stop raining! But it did at last; and when Ponto and Tabby ran down the hill again, they saw at the bottom—a pond deep enough to drown them both!

Tabby did not know what to do. In all her travels she had never crossed a pond of water. She was frightened, and would have gone back to the house, but she looked toward the barn, and saw Mary and the pan of milk waiting for her beside the door.

Ponto did not care for the water, for he could swim. So when they came to the edge of the pond, he plunged in and was soon across. Then he looked back to see what had become of Tabby. He thought she would be at his heels.

But no! There she was on the bank where he had left her. Her back was curled up till it looked as if it were broken, and her tail was

waving over it! What in the world was the matter? She never looked so except when she was angry.

Now, Ponto thought Tabby was a wonderful cat. He had seen her catch rats, and he knew that she could do some things that even he could not. "Surely she can cross that pond," thought he. He did not know what to make of it.

He called to her, with a bark, to "Jump in and swim across." But she only replied with a cross "Meouw," which he did not hear. Then he said again, "It's easy to swim across—come on!"

"As easy as for you to climb a tree," said Tabby, in an angry way.

This was too much for Ponto! He could not climb a tree, and Tabby knew it. When he was too rough in his play, she would run up into the apple-tree, and there she was safe. So this reply made him angry. Tabby should not have said it—but then, she wanted the milk!

"It is so easy that I can swim across and carry you, too," thought Ponto, and then he plunged into the water again. When he reached the shore, he seized Tabby by the back of the neck with his teeth, and rushed back into the water. Poor Tabby! She thought she certainly would be drowned. But Ponto knew better. He held his head so high that the water hardly touched her pretty little paws. So she kept quiet and did not struggle. It was not so bad after all! And besides, there was the milk!

When they landed, Tabby had a stiff neck for a while, and Ponto had to shake his great shaggy sides until they were dry. Then they ran up the hill as fast as they could go, and into the barn,—and almost into the milk-pail before they could stop.

Tabby was very thankful to Ponto for this ride. She said to herself that she would help him to climb a tree the next time that he tried. But as she drank her milk, she was glad that they both could follow Mary home by the long path through the orchard.

Tabby did not forget her strange ride. But she has never taught Ponto how to climb a tree! She has not even helped him up to the lowest limb. Do you think she ever will?

GOING TO THE MOON.

It is very easy to go up a big hill, but what would you think of any one who proposed to go to the moon? Once there was a man who wished to go, and he thought and thought and thought about it, till at last he dreamed that he was going! His dream was very pleasant indeed, but just as he was climbing up the long stairs of the moon-station with all the other passengers, he woke up, and that was the end of his wonderful voyage.

"ALL ABOARD FOR THE MOON!"

SAID a hazy little, mazy little, lazy little boy:
"To see the windmill working so must every one annoy;
It can be stopped, I'm sure it can, and so I'd like to know,
What in the world can ever make a windmill want to go?"

Said a quizzy little, frizzy little, busy little girl:
"What can be more delightful than to see a windmill whirl?
It loves to go, I'm sure it does, and hates to hang ker-flop;
Now, what on earth can ever make a windmill want to stop?"

One day, Grand-ma went to sleep in her chair, and it near-ly turned the town up-side down. It was only a lit-tle bit of a nap, but oh! how much trou-ble it made!

You see, be-sides the nap, there was a lit-tle boy in the house. This lit-tle boy's name was Rob, and Rob was so hard to watch that when his Mam-ma went out she used to say:

"Grand-ma, *do* you think you can watch Rob while I go to mar-ket?"

Then Grand-ma would give a lit-tle jump and say:

"O! of course I can."

So this day Mam-ma went to mar-ket, and Grand-ma watched Rob as hard as she could till the NAP came!

As soon as Rob saw the nap, he knew he was free; and off he ran.

In a mo-ment Grand-ma woke up and saw the emp-ty room.

"Sake's a-live!" she cried, as she ran out in-to the hall. "Where is that child?"

He was not in the hall, nor in the yard, nor any-where a-bout the house. Oh! oh! oh! where could he be!

The poor old la-dy was sure she nev-er would see the dear boy a-gain. In her fright she looked in the beds, un-der

the beds, in the pan-try, in the coal-scut-tle, in the ice-pitch-er, and even in the crack-er-box. Then she ran out to a po-lice-man, and told him all a-bout it.

"Mad-am," said the po-lice-man, "it is not like-ly he can be found. I think he is gone for good; but we'll send a cri-er all over the town."

So the cri-er went all over the town with a big bell, scream-ing:

"Hear! hear! Boy lost, named Rob,—black eyes, pug nose. Boy lost! boy lost!" (Ding, dong.) "Boy lost, three years old!" (Ding, dong.)

The cri-er made such a noise that if Rob had screamed out "Here I am!" right un-der his nose, he would not have heard it; or if all the men on the street had called, "Stop that bell—here's Rob, safe and sound," it would have been just the same. He would have gone on ring-ing the bell and scream-ing at the top of his voice, "Boy lost! boy lost!"

But Rob was not un-der the boy's nose at all. Where was he?

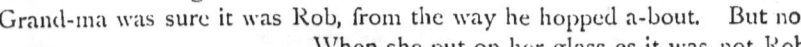

Poor Grand-ma was al-most cra-zy by this time. She ran in-to the yard with a kind man and looked down the well.

"Rob-by! Rob-by, my dar-ling! are you there? Come to Grand-ma, my pet. Oh! oh!"

Then she ran back in-to the street, and there he was with an or-gan man!

Grand-ma was sure it was Rob, from the way he hopped a-bout. But no. When she put on her glass-es it was not Rob at all—only a mon-key.

By this time near-ly the whole town knew that Rob was lost. Such a time you nev-er heard. All the grand-mas cried and said it was very wrong to take a nap when you were watch-ing a child like that; and all the lit-tle boys thought how nice it would be to live with Rob's grand-ma. The pa-pas went to the sta-tion-house to in-quire; the mam-mas ran to mar-ket to tell Rob's mam-ma; and the news-boys ran all o-ver town with "ex-tras," cry-ing, "Boy lost! boy lost!"

When Rob's mam-ma heard the bad news, she ran home as fast as she could go.

"Rob-by! Rob-by!" she called, up and down the house. "Rob-by! Rob-by!" But no one an-swered. Then she turned pale, and Grand-ma said, "Don't faint; that's a good child," when all at once the poor

Mam-ma clasped her hands and said: "He must be killed! If he were a-live he would hear me. I know he must be dead, or else—or else—he is eat-ing jam!"

She flew to the cel-lar where all the good things were kept. Grand-ma hob-bled after her, quite tired out; then fol-lowed the po-lice-man, the cri-er, and the cook; and there, down in the cel-lar, just as hap-py as he could be, sat Rob—eat-ing jam.

He was so hap-py that he did not know that his Grand-ma was a-wake; and Grand-ma was so glad that she went up-stairs and took the nicest lit-tle nap she ev-er had in all her life.

THE OLD MAN BY THE GATE.

An old man who lived by a gate,
On the passers-by promptly would wait;
  And when no one would ride,
  He would open it wide,
And march through himself in great state.

KITE-TIME.

WHAT AND WHERE?

MISCHIEVOUS Tommy,
  He hears every day
A long list of warnings
  Beginning this way:
"Now, Tommy, you must n't";
  And "Tommy, you must";
And "Tommy, stop running;
  You 'll kick up the dust";
And "Do not go swim-
    ming
  Or you will get wet";
And "Do not go sailing
  Or you will upset";

And "Do not be wrestling,
  You 'll fracture your bones";
And "Do not go climbing,
  You 'll fall on the stones";
And "Do not be whistling,
  You 're not a mere bird";
And "Good little children
  Are seen and not heard."

Which Tommy on hearing
  Exclaims, "Deary me!
What *can* a boy do,
  And where *can* a boy be?"

AN OLD STORY RETOLD.

Once upon a time a cat and a rat lived together in an old brick oven that was no more used. One day the cat was spinning, and the rat, to plague her, bit off her thread. The cat looked very cross at the rat and said in a loud voice, "If you bite off my thread again I'll hide away your small baby rat." The rat waited till the cat spun out a thread of great length when he jumped up and bit it off. Pussy sprang at the little rat quick as a flash and ran away with it. The rat began to cry and said, "Please, Mrs. Cat, bring back my dear little rat again." The cat said: "I will, if you will go to the cow and get me some milk."

So away he went, trit-a-tee trot,
The faster he went the further he got,

and said, "Cow, please give me milk: I will give Puss the milk; and Puss will give me my dear little rat again." The cow said, "I will, if you will go to the barn and get me some hay."

So away he went, trit-a-tee trot,
The faster he went the further he got,

and said, "Blacksmith, please give me the key: I will give Barn the key; Barn will give

me hay; I will give Cow the hay; Cow will give me milk; I will give Puss the milk; and Puss will give me my dear little rat again." The blacksmith said, "I will, if you will go to the coal-bank and get me some coal."

So away he went, trit-a-tee trot,
The faster he went the further he got,

and said, "Coal-bank, please give me some coal: I will give Blacksmith coal; Blacksmith will give me the key; I will give Barn the key; Barn will give me hay; I will give Cow the hay; Cow will give me milk; I will give Puss the milk, and Puss will give me my dear little rat again." The coal-bank said, "I will, if you will go to the brook and get me some water."

So away he went, trit-a-tee trot,

The faster he went the further he got,

and said, "Brook, please give me some water: I will give Coal-bank the water; Coal-bank will give me coal; I will give Blacksmith the coal; Blacksmith will give me the key; I will give Barn the key; Barn will give me hay; I will give Cow the hay; Cow will give me milk; I will give Puss the milk; and Puss will give me my dear little rat again."

The brook was good and kind, and had just been laughing to itself because it was so happy; and it was glad to have the chance to help the poor, tired, lonely rat. So the brook gave the water to the rat, and he gave it to the coal-bank; and the coal-bank gave the coal to the rat, and he gave it to the blacksmith; the blacksmith gave the key to the rat, and he gave it to the barn; the barn gave hay to the rat, and he gave it to the cow; the cow gave the milk to the rat, and he gave it to the cat; and then Mrs. Puss brought back to the rat the dear little rat again, and the rat never bit off her thread any more, but was a quiet, good rat ever after.

Margaret R. Gorseline.

EARLY AND LATE.

By W. S. Reed.

Go to bed early — wake up with joy;
Go to bed late — cross girl or boy.
Go to bed early — ready for play;
Go to bed late — moping all day.
Go to bed early — no pains or ills;
Go to bed late — doctors and pills.

A RAINY DAY.

HOW DID SHE KNOW?
(*A True Story.*)

By Caroline Evans.

In little Daisy's dimpled hand two bright, new pennies shone;
One was for Rob (at school just then), the other Daisy's own.
While waiting Rob's return she rolled both treasures round the floor,
When suddenly they disappeared, and one was seen no more.
"Poor Daisy! Is your penny lost?" was asked in accents kind.
"Why, no, *mine's* here!" she quickly said. "It's Rob's I cannot find."

BICYCLE SONG.

By Harriet Prescott Spofford.

Light upon the pedal,
   Firm upon the seat,
Swift, oh, swift and silent,
   Rolling down the street!

Bells before us tinkling,
   Fairily and sweet,
We're gliding, rolling, whirling
   Through the startled street!

Swift, oh, swift and silent,—
   And just before we meet
The outer edge of nothing
   We turn, rolling up the street!

LIT-TLE RED HEN.

(The Good Old Story of " the Little Red Hen and the Grain of Wheat," told in verse.)

By Eudora M. Bumstead.

Lit-tle Red Hen looked bus-i-ly round
　In search of a bit to eat,
Till, hid in the straw and chaff, she found
　A plump lit-tle grain of wheat.
"Now, who will plant this wheat?" she cried.
"Not I!" the goose and the duck re-plied;
"Not I!" said the dog and the cat;
"Not I!" said the mouse and the rat.
"Oh, I will, then!" said Lit-tle Red Hen,
　And scratched with her quick lit-tle feet
Till a hole she dug, and cov-ered it snug,
　And so she plant-ed the wheat.

Lit-tle Red Hen gave ten-der care,
　The rain and the shine came down,
And the wheat grew green and tall and fair,
　Then turned to a gold-en brown.
"Now, who will reap this wheat?" she cried.
"Not I!" the goose and the duck re-plied;
"Not I!" said the dog and the cat;
"Not I!" said the mouse and the rat.
"Oh, I will, then!" said Lit-tle Red Hen;
　And, brav-ing the mid-sum-mer heat,
She cut it at will with her trim lit-tle bill,
　And so she reaped the wheat.

Lit-tle Red Hen peeped sly-ly a-bout
　From her snug lit-tle nest in the hay;
If only that wheat were all threshed out,
　And fit to be stored a-way.
"Now, who will thresh this wheat?" she cried.
"Not I!" the goose and the duck re-plied;
"Not I!" said the dog and the cat;
"Not I!" said the mouse and the rat.

"Oh, I will, then!" said Lit-tle Red Hen;
  And, hav-ing no flail, she beat
With her wings of red on the grain, in-stead,
  And so she threshed the wheat.

Lit-tle Red Hen had still no rest,
  Al-though she had worked so well;
She thought of the chicks in her snug lit-tle nest,
  How soon they would peep in the shell.
"Now, who will go to the
  mill?" she cried.
"Not I!" the goose and
  the duck re-plied;

"Not I!" said the dog and the cat;
"Not I!" said the mouse and the rat.
"Oh, I will, then!" said Lit-tle Red Hen,
  And fashioned a sack so neat,

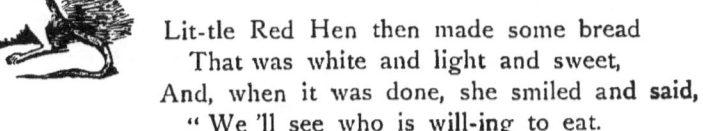

  With corn-silk thread and a corn-husk red,
    In which she car-ried the wheat.

Lit-tle Red Hen then made some bread
  That was white and light and sweet,
And, when it was done, she smiled and said,
  "We'll see who is will-ing to eat.
"Now, who will eat this loaf?" she cried.
"I will," the goose and the duck re-plied;
    "I will!" said the dog and the cat;
    "I will!" said the mouse and the rat.
"No doubt!" said the hen, "if you get it!" and then
  (How the lazy rogues longed for the treat!)
She clucked to her chicks — she was moth-er of six;
  And that was the end of the wheat.

A WARRIOR BOLD.

THE TURKEY'S NEST.

By Frank H. Sweet.

"If you find the nest," said Farmer Brown,
  With a twinkle in his eye,
"You shall have the nicest thing in town
  That a dollar bill will buy.
But, mind you, it won't be children's play,
  For that sly old turkey-hen
Has often stolen her nest away,
  And has puzzled all my men."

Across the fields and into the wood,
  And down by the running brook,
Among the logs where the old mill stood,
  Into every kind of nook,
And, one by one, they gave up the quest—
  Bobbie and Jack and Fred.
"We never could find that turkey's nest,
  If we searched a month," they said.

The fields were wide and the hills were steep
  And the baby's years were few,
And she lagged behind and went to sleep
  Where the alder-bushes grew.
And the turkey did not see her guest,
  As she sought her eggs to set;
So baby awoke and found the nest—
  And the folks are wondering yet.

WHY CHERRIES GROW.

By Clinton Scollard.

"Why do cherries grow?"
  Said I; "Robin red,
  Chirping overhead
In the gleam and glow,—
Why do cherries grow?"

Paused he perkishly
  While he plucked at one
  Flushing in the sun;
Then said he, said he,
"Cherries grow for me!"

ENOUGH FOR TWO.

THE BABY'S SUNNY CORNER
DRAWN BY MARY HALLOCK FOOTE.

BABY'S JOURNEY.

Hop-pet-y, hop-pet-y, ho!
Where shall the ba-by go?
O-ver dale and down,
To Lim-er-ick town,
And there shall the ba-by go.

Hop-pet-y, hop-pet-y, ho!
How shall the ba-by go?
In a coach and four,
And pos-si-bly more,
And so shall the ba-by go.

Hop-pet-y, hop-pet-y, ho!
When shall the ba-by go?
In the aft-er-noon,
By the light of the moon,
And then shall the ba-by go.

Hop-pet-y, hop-pet-y, ho!
Why shall the ba-by go?
To learn a new jig,
And to buy a new wig,
And that's why the ba-by shall **go.**

TILTING.

Tilt away, my little men,
Out on Grandpa's lawn again;
Jack is up, and Fred is down,
It makes one laugh, the other frown,—
Like our changeful summer weather.

"Well, never mind, just tilt it back,
Up comes Fred, and down goes Jack!
Up and down, this is the way
The sport goes on, the livelong day,
When two wee boys would tilt together."

THE GIN-GER-BREAD BOY.

Now you shall hear a sto-ry that some-bod-y's great, great-grand-moth-er told a lit-tle girl ev-er so ma-ny years a-go:

There was once a lit-tle old man and a lit-tle old wom-an, who lived in a lit-tle old house in the edge of a wood. They would have been a ver-y hap-py old coup-le but for one thing,—they had no lit-tle child, and they wished for one ver-y much. One day, when the lit-tle old wom-an was bak-ing gin-ger-bread, she cut a cake in the shape of a lit-tle boy, and put it in-to the ov-en.

Pres-ent-ly, she went to the ov-en to see if it was baked. As soon as the ov-en door was o-pened, the lit-tle gin-ger-bread boy jumped out, and be-gan to run a-way as fast as he could go.

The lit-tle old wom-an called her hus-band, and they both ran aft-er him. But they could not catch him. And soon the gin-ger-bread boy came to a barn full of thresh-ers. He called out to them as he went by, say-ing:

> "I've run a-way from a lit-tle old wom-an,
> A lit-tle old man,
> And I can run a-way from you, I can!"

Then the barn full of thresh-ers set out to run aft-er him. But, though they ran fast, they could not catch him. And he ran on till he came to a field full of mow-ers. He called out to them:

> "I've run a-way from a lit-tle old wom-an,
> A lit-tle old man,
> A barn full of thresh-ers,
> And I can run a-way from you, I can!"

Then the mow-ers be-gan to run aft-er him, but they could n't catch him. And he ran on till he came to a cow. He called out to her:

"I 've run a-way from a lit-tle old wom-an,
    A lit-tle old man,
    A barn full of thresh-ers,
    A field full of mow-ers,
And I can run a-way from you, I can!"

But, though the cow start-ed at once, she could n't catch him. And soon he came to a pig. He called out to the pig:

"I 've run a-way from a lit-tle old wom-an,
    A lit-tle old man,
    A barn full of thresh-ers,
    A field full of mow-ers,
    A cow,—
And I can run a-way from you, I can!"

But the pig ran, and could n't catch him. And he ran till he came a-cross a fox, and to him he called out:

"I 've run a-way from a lit-tle old wom-an,
    A lit-tle old man,
    A barn full of thresh-ers,
    A field full of mow-ers,
    A cow and a pig,
And I can run a-way from you, I can!"

Then the fox set out to run. Now fox-es can run ver-y fast, and so the fox soon caught the gin-ger-bread boy and be-gan to eat him up.

Pres-ent-ly the gin-ger-bread boy said: "O dear! I'm quar-ter gone!" And then: "Oh, I'm half gone!" And soon: "I'm three-quar-ters gone!" And at last: "I'm all gone!" and nev-er spoke a-gain.

THE GOOD BOY BRIGADE.

THE MIDNIGHT EXPRESS.

THE ROBBER RAT AND THE POOR LITTLE KITTEN.

By Katharine Pyle.

I.

A KITTEN once lived all alone
  In a little yellow house;
It lived on crusts of bread and cheese,
  And now and then a mouse.

III.

To the yellow house the rat would come,
  And strike the door—knock! knock!
The kitten's tail would stand on end,
  It gave him such a shock.

II.

A robber rat lived in a wood—
  A gloomy wood—close by;
He had sharp teeth, and a pointed tail,
  And a wicked, restless eye.

IV.

Then in the rat would boldly march.
  "What have you here?" he'd say;
And then he would steal the bread and cheese
  And carry it all away.

THE ROBIN.

By Anna Chase Davis.

I AM going to tell you a story about the robin. All the children love him and know him by his pretty red breast. He comes to see us in the spring. We are glad to hear his sweet song.
We are sure then that the warm days are near.
His little mate and he choose a place for their home.
Then they build their nest.
Do they build in a high tree or a low bush?
Watch them and you will see.
It is such hard work for them.
See how busy they are.
They have to carry everything in their beaks and claws.
Would you like to help them?
I will tell you how you can do it.
Cut some pieces of string about six inches long.
Measure six inches and you will see how long that is.
Scatter the pieces of string on the grass.
Now watch the robins.
They will soon find the string.
They like it to put in their nest.
If you find an old nest some day, you will see some bits of string in it.
See how well it is made.
Could you make one like it?
Who teaches the birds to build their nests?
The robin's nest is lined with mud. To make it smooth and round, the mother-bird gets into the nest. Then she turns round and round. She **uses** her breast for this. Now the nest is finished.
What does the mother-bird do next?
She lays her eggs in the nest.
What color are they?
How many are there?

Does the mother-bird leave the eggs? No; she sits on them to keep them warm. She flies off for food. She stays only a short time.

Soon little baby-birds will come out of those eggs. If the eggs should get cold the baby-birds would die.

The father-bird comes and sings to the mother-bird. She is very patient. Day after day she sits there.

In about two weeks she hears a little pecking sound. The baby-birds are knocking to come out. Soon the shells crack and the birds are in the nest.

How glad the old birds are! They are busy now getting food for their babies. See how they get the worms for their breakfast.

The young birds grow stronger every day. They are not pretty when they are little.

WATCHING THE ROBINS.

FINDING THE BITS OF STRING.

Soon the feathers grow longer and thicker. Now they are strong enough to fly.

They stand on the edge of the nest. They are *so* afraid!

The father and mother fly about them. They chirp and call to them.

I suppose they tell the little ones not to be afraid.

Soon they will fly away.

Robins are of the kind of birds called "perchers."

See how many toes they have. How many in front? how many behind? Their feet are made to hop from twig to twig. They perch on the branches. Their claws are long so that they can clasp the branch. What color are the robins? Are the mother-bird and father-bird the same color? Watch them and see.

> One day an ant went to visit her neighbor;
> She found her quite busy with all sorts of labor;
> So she did n't go in, but stopped at the sill,
> Left her respects, and went back to her hill.

HOW ROB COUNTED THE STARS.

Oth-er lit-tle boys have count-ed the stars, but let me tell you how lit-tle Rob count-ed them. Rob was then just four years old.

It was a warm sum-mer night. Mam-ma had put Rob in-to bed, and aft-er kiss-ing him sev-er-al times, had left him a-lone to fall a-sleep. The stars came out, one by one, till the win-dow was full of the lit-tle bright twink-lers, and the tired lit-tle boy lay won-der-ing at their bright-ness, and count-ing them on his fin-gers and toes; but pret-ty soon ev-er-y lit-tle fin-ger and toe was "used up," and Rob had ma-ny

stars left in the win-dow and no-where to put them. "If I on-ly had a lit-tle sis-ter," he said, "I could use her fin-gers." And there he lay, with his arms stretched up-ward and a star on ev-er-y lit-tle fin-ger-tip. Then a hap-py thought came in-to his head. He popped out of the bed, and in an in-stant more was mak-ing a map of the lit-tle piece of sky which he saw, by put-ting a mark for ev-er-y star up-on his slate. But soon he grew dream-y, his pen-cil moved slow-er, and slow-er, and lit-tle Rob was fast a-sleep.

The next morn-ing, Rob's mam-ma found the slate ly-ing by his side, cov-ered with queer lit-tle marks, but mam-ma did n't know what they were till Rob said they were **stars**, and she could count them.

Can you make stars up-on your slate?

THE DIFFERENCE BETWEEN UP AND DOWN.

1.—IT'S SUCH WORK TO GO UP,—UP,—UP!

2.—BUT SUCH FUN TO GO DOWN,—DOWN,—DOWN!

PUSSY'S LESSON.

By C. D. L.

LISTEN, children, listen, and I will tell you true,
About a little pussy, and 't was —
    Mew, mew, mew!
Just as black as midnight, with long and silky fur,
Happy as the sunshine, and 't was —
    Purr, purr, purr.

One day when his mama was purring sound asleep,
Slyly stole this pussy, and 't was —
    Creep, creep, creep.
Jumped up on the pantry shelf, in the milk fell flat,
Wakened up his mama, and 't was —
    Scat, scat, scat!

Down she dragged him from the shelf, white as snowball now;
Boxed his ears with vigor, and 't was —
    Me-ow, me-ow, me-ow!

Now his mama's slumbers are sweet and calm to her —
Pussy minds his mama, and 't is —
    Purr, purr, purr.

Four little Pigs

One little pig planned
                to go out shopping;
One to walk by the
                brooklet's side;
One intended to play
                lawn-tennis;
One decided a wheel
                to ride.

The hired man came with a
                bag of apples;
"Piggy! piggy!" they heard
                him call.
Helter-skelter they went back,
                squealing;
"Home is the best place,
                after all!"

A TENDER-HEARTED ARAB.

By Frederick B. Opper.

Said Ali Ben Hassan, a kind-hearted man,
"I 'll treat my poor camel as well as I can.

"It is such a hot day, I will shade the poor fellow
With my second-best, apple-green cotton umbrella.

"With a pair of blue goggles I 'll shield his poor eyes
From the glare of the sun, and I 'll keep off the flies

"And cool him, at times, with my big palm-leaf fan!"
Said Ali Ben Hassan, a kind-hearted man.

LITTLE PERI-WINKLE.

LITTLE Peri-Winkle,
With her eyes a-twinkle,
Said, "I am going to the ball to-night."
But nobody could wake her,
Hard as they might shake her,
For she went to sleep with her eyes shut tight,
And never waked up till the sun shone bright.

THE OWL, THE EEL, AND THE WARMING-PAN.

THE owl and the eel and the warming-pan,
They went to call on the soap-fat man.
The soap-fat man, he was not within;
He'd gone for a ride on his rolling-pin;
So they all came back by the way of the town,
And turned the meeting-house upside down.

PUNKYDOODLE AND JOLLAPIN.

OH, Pillykin Willykin Winky Wee!
How does the Emperor take his tea?
He takes it with melons, he takes it with milk,
He takes it with syrup and sassafras silk.
He takes it without, he takes it within;
Oh, Punkydoodle and Jollapin!

THE KITTENS' PICNIC.

A RHYME FOR VERY LITTLE FOLK.

In her nest on the limb of an apple-tree a mother Robin sat,
When the father Robin came in haste to say, "I've seen a cat!
A smallish cat — a kitten, in fact, that's coming toward our tree.
He seems to be bringing a basket. What can the reason be?"

"A kitten?" she cried — "a crowd of them! For, see, there come some
    more!"
And she was right, for very soon the Robins counted a score —
Carrying baskets, cans, a net — a wagon-load, at least,
Of things that smelled so very good they surely meant a feast.
Robins don't love cats, you know, and so they flew away,
For they saw 't was a Kittens' Picnic that had come to stay all day.

The Kittens chose that very spot to spread their cloth so white,
But set up the lawn-tennis net where the sun shone warm and bright.
The youngsters then chased butterflies, or danced in a merry ring,
Or just beneath the Robins' nest enjoyed a lazy swing,
Until it was time to be hungry, when out came tiny dishes
With a toothsome pie, cool lemonade, sweet candy, jam, and fishes.

A little chap in a dotted shirt (a favorite, it would seem)
Was chosen by his comrades as the one to serve ice-cream.
He counted every kitten, dividing the cream with care,
So not one kitten had too much, while each one had his share.
This pleased them all, and they declared he was "a little brick!"
And all agreed that he deserved the ice-cream spoon to lick.
How prettily he purred his thanks for this reward unsought,
How glad he was that he had done as a kindly kitten ought!

Now when the lunch was eaten the sun had sunk so low
That all the older kittens announced 't was time to go.
The youngsters whined a little, but knew they must obey,
And packing up their things again the kittens went away.

As soon as the last little furry tail was fairly out of sight
Back came the timid Robins to their nest to spend the night.
But, best of all, for many a day the happy Robins found
A feast for their nestlings in the crumbs of the Kittens' picnic-ground.

MORAL.

So many a present trouble, that seems but to annoy,
May bring you on a future day a pleasure to enjoy.

The Ballad of a runaway Donkey:
by Emilie Poulsson:
[Abridged for Baby World.]

pictures by Alfred Brenon.

A sturdy little Donkey,
All dressed in sober gray,
Once took it in his long-eared head
That he would run away.

So, when a little open
He saw the stable door,
He ran as if he never would
Come back there any more.

Away that Donkey galloped
And ran and ran and ran
And ran and ran and ran and ran
And Ran and RAn and RAN!

And he *never* came back!

MARCH—

THE BRIGHT SIDE.

NANNY has a hopeful way—
   Bright and busy Nanny.
When I cracked the cup to-day,
She said in her hopeful way,
"It's only cracked — don't fret, I pray."
   Sunny, cheery Nanny!

Nanny has a hopeful way,
   So good and sweet and canny.
When I broke the cup to-day,
She said in her hopeful way,
"Well, 't was *cracked*, I'm glad to say."
   Kindly, merry Nanny!

Nanny has a hopeful way—
   Quite right, little Nanny.
Cups will crack and break alway;
Fretting does n't mend or pay.
Do the best you can, I say,
   Busy, loving Nanny.

—AND APRIL.

GRANDMAMA.

By Helen Hopkins.

Mother says, "You mischievous girl!
  You're busier than a bee!"
And father says, "Go play, my dear,
  And don't be bothering *me!*"

But grandmama says, "You blessed lamb!
  The darling of my heart!—
Eliza, I think she wants some jam,
  Or a cake and an apple tart."

HOW THEY RIDE.

By Eva L. Carson.

BRAVELY comes the gentleman,
Trotting nimbly as he can;
Lifts his hat to Meg and Dot
As he passes — trot, trot, trot.

Now the postboy follows fast,
Gallop, gallop — ah, he's past,
Spares not spur, but shakes the rein,
Gallops on with might and main.

Next there comes the country boy,
Many a jump, and hobbledy-hoy.
Bumpety-bump! — if he fall down,
Ten to one he cracks his crown!

This is the way the ladies ride,
Gently pacing, side by side,
Backward and forward, to and fro,
See, my darling, how they go.

Pace, and gallop, and trot, my dear,
So they've traveled for many a year;
But none of them all can happier be
Than Goldilocks on her father's knee

"GO 'WAY! GO 'WAY! THEY 'RE FLOWERS!"

"WHAT TIME DOES PAPA COME?"

HALLOA, OLD SCUTTLE!

Halloa, old scuttle! good old soul,
What's become of all your coal?
"Why, the tongs he came with a gobbledy-gun,
And took my coals out, one by one;
And the blaze ran in with a tricksy-spire
And set the pretty things afire;
And the blower came with a roaring roar,
And made them burn up more and more;
And the poker with kloppity-hop,
He poked their ashes and made 'em drop,—
And that, O Gobbledy-kloppity-dole!
Is what's become of all my coal."

There was a small servant called Kate,
Who sat on the stairs very late;
When asked how she fared,
She said she was scared,
But was otherwise doing first rate.

NUMBER ONE.

"I TELL you," said Robbie, eating his peach,
   And giving his sister none,
"I believe in the good old saying that each
   Should look out for Number One."

"Why, yes," answered Katie, wise little elf,
   "But the counting should be begun
With the *other one*, instead of yourself,—
   And *he* should be Number One."

HOW THE SLIDE WAS SPOILED.

ONE Friday there was a heavy fall of snow, and some small boys and girls laid plans for a good time on Saturday. They made a great many snow-balls, and piled them in heaps ready for the next day. They made a slide down the side of a little hill, jumping on the snow until it was smooth and hard, and then poured pails of water over the slide to make it icy and slippery. All was done by dinner-time, and the children ran home, thinking how much fun they would have on Saturday.

No sooner were the children gone than a little bear passed that way. It was his birthday, and he had on his best coat and trousers, but he had not had any presents. Mr. and Mrs. Bruin had meant to give him some honeycomb, but the farmer who kept bees bought a big dog about that time, and Mr. and Mrs. Bruin could not get the honey for their son Smiler.

So Smiler Bruin was a little cross, and was walking about the woods and growling to himself. But when he came to the slide that the children had made, and saw the piles of snow-balls, he lost his ill humor, and was very glad. "Oh!" he cried, "how kind of somebody! They made this nice slide for a surprise. I will give a party and ask all my friends." He ran off, as fast as he could go through the deep snow, and told all the little bears he knew to come to his Slide and Snowball Party. Ten of them could come, and trotted after Smiler, who led the way, as proud as he could be.

The water had frozen on the slide, and it was as smooth as any little bear-cub could wish. All said that Smiler should have the first slide; and, taking a good run, he spread his legs wide apart, and sailed grandly down the hill, while all the little bears clapped their paws and growled joyfully.

But, when Smiler came to the foot of the hill, his claws hit a branch that was just under the top of the snow, and Smiler went paws over nose into a deep drift, and had to be pulled out by the heels.

Then the little bears went down the slide, one by one, as fast as they could go. And they threw all the snowballs at each other. Every time a bear was hit, he did not like it much; but all the others did, so he had to laugh. Well!—when Smiler's birthday party was over the children's snow-balls were all smashed, and the slide was all scratched up, and the children never knew who did it.

I had a little row boat.
It was called the "Mary Jane"
And I always kept it fastened
To the boat house by a chain.

But it somehow got afloat one day
And drifted out to sea,
And now I often wonder where
The "Mary Jane" can be.

They were happy and did laugh
When their friend, the big Giraffe,
Said, "I'll take you to the City,
    in a tandem."
But their joy was turned to grief
When their charger bit a leaf,
Never thinking how his sudden stop
    would land 'em

SCENE I.

SCENE II.

PAINTING A CARD FOR MOTHER'S BIRTHDAY.

"NOW" AND "WAITAWHILE."

By Nixon Waterman.

LITTLE Jimmie Waitawhile and little Johnnie Now
Grew up in homes just side by side; and that, you see, is how
I came to know them both so well, for almost every day
I used to watch them at their work and also at their play.

Little Jimmie Waitawhile was bright, and sturdy, too,
But never ready to perform what he was asked to do;
"Wait just a minute," he would say, "I'll do it pretty soon,"
And things he should have done at morn were never done till noon.

He put off studying until his boyhood days were gone;
He put off getting him a home till age came stealing on;

He put off everything, and so his life was not a joy,
And all because he waited "just a minute" while a boy.

But little Johnnie Now would say, when he had work to do:
"There's no time like the present time," and gaily put it through.
And when his time for play arrived he so enjoyed the fun;
His mind was not distressed with thoughts of duties left undone.

In boyhood he was studious and laid him out a plan
Of action to be followed when he grew to be a man;
And life was as he willed it all because he'd not allow
His tasks to be neglected, but would always do them "now."

And so in every neighborhood are scores of little boys,
Who by and by must work with tools when they have done with toys.
And you know one of them, I guess, because I see you smile;
And is he little Johnnie Now, or Jimmie Waitawhile?

MARJORIE: "UPSET ME IF YOU DARE! PLEASE DON'T!"

Sunday, sixpence in the plate;
Monday, makes the scholars late;
Tuesday, work is well begun;
Wednesday, leaves the lazy one;
Thursday, full as full can be;
Friday, friends come in for tea;
Saturday, the kitchen clean; —
Sunday comes for rest between.

WEE little house with the golden thatch;
Twice I knocked and I lifted the latch:
  "And pray, is the mistress here?"
"In black stuff gown and a yellow vest,
She's busily packing her honey-chest;
  Will you taste a bit, my dear?"

A BOBOLINK and a chick-a-dee
Sang a sweet duet in the apple-tree.
"When I'm in good voice," said the chick-a-lee,
"I sing like you to 'high' C, 'high' C;
But I've caught such a cold
That for love or for gold
I can sing only chick-a-dee-dee-dee-dee!"

MY LADY IS EATING HER MUSH.

HUSHABY, hushaby, hush,
My lady is eating her mush.
Her little black servant, alas!
Is bobbing in front of the glass—
Bobbing now, just think upon it,
Dressed in my lady's best bonnet!

The cat on the pantry shelf
To the cream is helping herself.
A little gray mouse, at her ease,
Is nibbling away at the cheese.
Each slyly her own way pursuing,
Sees not what the other is doing;—

But wait till my lady is done!
Wait, if you wish to see fun!

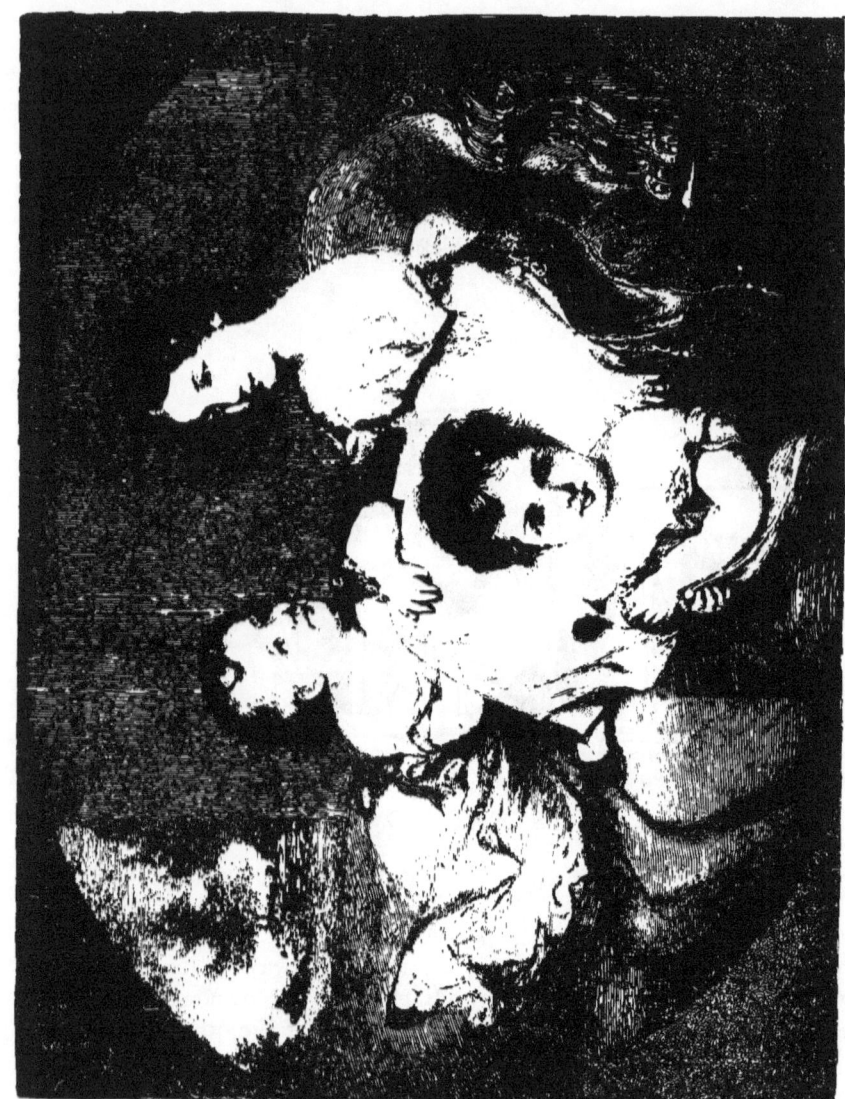

THREE LITTLE SISTERS.
FROM A PAINTING BY WILLIAM PAGE

By M. M. D.

One day little Bertie Green came running in from the garden. She held something in her apron, but no one could see what it was. "Oh, mamma," she said, "let's play three wishes. Play you're a poor woman and I'm a be-yoo-ti-ful fairy. Will you, mamma?"

Mamma laughed, and said she would try.

"Very well," said Bertie, "you'll see what a splendid game it is. Now, shut your eyes tight, we're going to begin! I'm a fairy, and I'll grant you three wishes. There's something in my apron, you know, mamma, but it's a secret. Now, *wish!*"

"Well," said mamma, closing her eyes, "let me think."

"That's right, mamma; wish for something real nice—a rose, or a cherry, or anything!"

"I wish for a rose," said her mamma, very slowly.

"Here it is!" cried Bertie, laughing with joy, and handing her mamma a lovely rose. "Now, wish again, mamma."

"Let——me——think," said mamma again. "Now, what *shall* I wish for?" "Something to eat!" the fairy hinted.

"Oh, yes; something to eat!" mamma said; "well, I wish——I wish for two nice cherries!"

"Good! good!" shouted Bertie, giving mamma a bright little red bunch. "How *did* you know? Are they sweet?"

"Yes, indeed," said mamma; "and I thank you very much, good fairy! But I can have another wish, you know!"

"Y-e-s!" said Bertie, looking troubled, and letting go of the little empty apron; "only, I don't know how to play any more wishes!"

"I do!" said mamma; "I wish for a kiss!" Then you should have seen the happy fairy climb up, throw her little arms around mamma's neck, and kiss her again and again!

"That was the very best wish of all," said mamma.

The Song of the Skipping Rope

Winter-time has fled away,
Spring has had her gentle sway,
Summer surely must be near
When the skipping-ropes appear;
    With a skip, skip, and a trip, trip,
      As thus we rise and fall;
      In yard and street the little feet
      Are coming to the call!

Oh, so many tricks to do
That our mothers also knew!—
"In the Front Door," "Baking Bread,"
"Chase the Fox," and "Needle Thread";
    With a skip, skip,
    And a trip, trip,—
    For so the leader saith—
      With a hop, jump,
      And a thump, thump,
    Until you're out of breath.

Hear the counting, sure and slow;
To a hundred they must go.
Not a hand or arm should swerve,
While the rope describes its curve;
    With a skip, skip, and a trip, trip,
      Until the task is done;
      With cheeks so red, and ruffled head,
      Bravo, my little one!

Boys may leap and vault so high,
But none was ever known to try
To master this soft, little spring
That is so quick and light a thing!
    With a skip, skip,
    And a trip, trip.
Oh, may I always hear
  That pit-pat-pit
  That seems to fit
The blossom-time of year!

IN TOP TIME.

By Henry Reeves.

THREE tops were lying in the ring;
  Three tip-top boys stood by;
Tip-tap! They flung their tops on top
  To make the others fly,—
When little Tim from Topping street
  With top in hand came nigh.

Said he: "I'll play at tops with you";
  "Good! Lay it down," said they.
So in the ring among the tops
  His little spinner lay.
Tip-tap! down came a heavy top
  And knocked the rest away.

It split the top of little Tim;
  Apart the pieces flew;
You'd think it was his heart that split,
  He made so much ado,—
"My top will never spin again—
  My top is split in two!"

The tip-top boys some pennies gave
  To Tim, and stopped his cry;
And off he ran to Topping street
  Another top to buy,—
A bright new top, a splendid top,
  A tip-top top to buy.

I LOOKED from my window,
  And dancing together,
I spied three queer people
  Who love the wet weather.
The turtle, the frog, and the duck all
  joined hands
To caper so gaily upon the wet sands.

  The turtle was coated
    In shell, to defy
  The pattering rain-drops,
    And keep him quite dry.

The frog in green jacket was gay as
  could be,
"My coat will shed water—just see it!"
  said he.

  The duck shook his web-feet
    And ruffled his feathers;
  Cried he, "Rain won't hurt me!
    I'm dressed for all weathers.
And when I can see the clouds frown
  in the sky
I oil my gray feathers and keep very dry!"

AT RECESS. THE DANCING BEAR.

BY M. M. D.

Ding-dong! ding-dong! ding!

The bell-ring-ers in the pict-ure are re-al cats. Their names are Jet, Blanche, Tom, Mop and Tib. Jet is Black; Blanche is white as snow; Tom stands in the mid-dle; Mop is next; and Tib, who has the small-est bell, has to reach high-est to ring it.

These five bright lit-tle cats—Jet, Blanche, Tom, Mop and Tib—have been trained to do won-der-ful tricks. They can stand up and beg like dogs; they can lie down and play that they are fast a-sleep; they can march in a row like sol-diers; more than all, they can ring the bells in good time, so soft-ly and sweet-ly that the music is pret-ty e-nough for Christ-mas chimes.

Mr. Bow-en tells a-bout them in a Lon-don book called "The Chil-dren's Friend." He says the mas-ter who taught them to ring the bells was al-ways ver-y kind and gen-tle. They knew that he loved them, and that when-ev-er they tried to learn their les-son well, he would give them a nice meal of fish.

Cats like fish as well as you like can-dy,—bet-ter than you like a can-dy fish; so you see they must have felt, when they gave the ropes a good pull, that, some-how, they were ring-ing their own din-ner-bell. At first the pus-sies found it ver-y hard to catch hold of the bell-rope; but when their mas-ter put soft bunch-es of wool up-on the cord, so that the pus-sies could fast-en their sharp lit-tle claws in-to it, they took hold with a good will.

"Ding-dong! Thank you, Mas-ter," they seemed to say. "This is some-thing like!"

Some-times the pus-sies would not a-gree ver-y well. Tib would get tired of her short rope, and try to get hold of Jet's. Then Blanche and Tom would join in the fight; the ropes would get twisted; all the bells would ring out of tune, and Mop would "me-ouw" with all her might. But the dread-ful noise would soon bring them to their senses; and the mo-ment they were good, the sweet mu-sic would come a-gain and make them hap-py.

When the pus-sies were not do-ing their fun-ny tricks, they would walk a-bout just like any oth-er cats, or lie down on the rug and doze. Some-times, in their sleep, they would wave their tails slow-ly, and then their mas-ter would say:

"Bless 'em! They are dream-ing of the bells."

If he called to them, they would spring to his side and rub their cool noses a-gainst his hand, or, jump-ing up-on his knee, they would look up in-to his face, as if to say:

"Good mas-ter! you look tired. Poor dear! you are on-ly a man. But you may de-pend up-on our help. We know ver-y well that if it were not for us cats there would be no bells rung in the world."

The mas-ter would smile at this, and stroke them fond-ly; then the fire-light would play a-bout their forms as, one by one, they would set-tle soft-ly up-on the rug for an-oth-er nap.

By M. L. van Vorst.

Over the crust of the hard white snow
The little feet of the reindeer go
(*Hush, hush, the winds are low*),
   And the fine little bells are ringing!
Nothing can reach thee of woe or harm —
Safe is the shelter of mother's arm
(*Hush, hush, the wind 's a charm*),
   And mother's voice is singing.

Father is coming — he rides apace;
Fleet are the steeds with the winds that race
(*Hush, hush, for a little space*);
   The snow to his mantle 's clinging.

His flying steed with the wind 's abreast —
Here by the fire are warmth and rest
(*Hush, hush, in your little nest*),
   And mother's voice is singing.

Over the crust of the snow, hard by,
The little feet of the reindeer fly
(*Hush, hush, the wind is high*),
   And the fine little bells are ringing!
Nothing can reach us of woe or harm —
Safe is the shelter of father's arm
(*Hush, hush, the wind 's a charm*),
   And mother's voice is singing.

"THE POOR LITTLE LAMB HAS BEEN RUNNING TOO HARD!"

WHAT COULD THE FARMER DO?

By George William Ogden.

There was an old farmer who had a cow,
   Moo, moo, moo!
She used to stand on the pump and bow,
   And what could the farmer do?
Moo, moo, moo, moo,
   Moo, moo, moo!
She used to stand on the pump and bow,
   And what could the farmer do?

There was an old farmer who owned some sheep,
   Baa, baa, baa!
They used to play cribbage while he was asleep,
   And laugh at the farmer's ma.
Baa, baa, baa, baa!
   Moo, moo, moo!
He owned a cow and he owned some sheep,
   And what could the poor man do?

There was an old farmer who owned a pig,
    Whoof, whoof, whoof!
He used to dress up in the farmer's wig,
    And dance on the pig-pen roof.
Whoof, whoof! Baa, baa!
    Moo, moo, moo!
He owned a pig, some sheep, and a cow,
    And what could the poor man do?

There was an old farmer who owned a hen,
    Cuk-a-ca-doo, ca-doo!
She used to lay eggs for the three hired men,
    And some for the weasel, too.
Cuk-a-ca-doo! Whoof, whoof!
    Baa, baa! Moo!
He owned a hen, pig, sheep, and a cow,
    And what could the poor man do?

There was an old farmer who had a duck,
    Quack, quack, quack!
She waddled under a two-horse truck
    For four long miles and back.
Quack, quack! Cuk-a-ca-doo!
    Whoof! Baa! Moo!
With a duck, hen, pig, a sheep, and a cow,
    Pray what could the poor man do?

There was an old farmer who had a cat,
 Mee-ow, mee-ow, mee-ow!
She used to waltz with a gray old rat
 By night in the farmer's mow.
Mee-ow! Quack! Cuk-a-ca-doo!
 Whoof! Baa! Moo!
With cat, duck, hen, pig, sheep, and a cow,
 Pray what could the poor man do?

EIGHT GOOD THINGS ABOUT DOBBIN.

Dobbin never would do us harm,
Dobbin takes us over the farm;
Dobbin follows us when we call;
Dobbin never will let us fall.
Dobbin is white as the whitest snow,
Dobbin shows even at night, you know.
Dobbin is patient, steady and kind;
Dobbin can teach us children to mind.
   Whether it's "Whoa! Dobbin,
     Dear old Dobbin,"
   Or "Go! Dobbin,
     Dear old Dobbin,"
Dobbin will mind, as a matter of course;
But everybody can't be a horse.
     Hey, Dobbin?

IS N'T IT QUEER?

By Mrs. H. M. Greenleaf.

Said A, "Whene'er I stand between
  The letters B and D,
I'm in the midst of all that's BAD,
  As you may plainly see."

"How strange!" said merry, laughing E;
  "When I between them am,
I'm tucked up comfortably in BED,
  And happy as a clam."

By Anna M. Pratt.

When it drizzles and drizzles,
  If we cheerfully smile,
We can make the weather,
By working together,
  As fair as we choose in a little while.
For who will notice that clouds are drear
If pleasant faces are always near,
And who will remember that skies are gray
If he carries a happy heart all day?

"I'VE BRINGED YOU A LITTLE DOLLY, BOSSY."

READY FOR HER FIRST DIP IN THE BIG OCEAN.

ALICE'S SUPPER.

Far down in the valley the wheat grows deep,
And the reapers are making the cradles sweep;
And this is the song that I hear them sing,
While cheery and loud their voices ring:
"'T is the finest wheat that ever did grow,
And it is for Alice's supper—ho! ho!"

Far down by the river the old mill stands,
And the miller is rubbing his dusty old hands;
And these are the words of the miller's lay,
As he watches the mill-stones grinding away:
"'T is the finest flour that money can buy,
And it is for Alice's supper—hi! hi!"

Down stairs in the kitchen the fire doth glow,
And cook is a-kneading the soft white dough;
And this is the song she is singing to-day,
As merry and busy she's working away:
"'T is the finest of dough whether near or afar,
And it is for Alice's supper—ha! ha!"

To the nursery now comes mother, at last,—
And what in her hand is she bringing so fast?
'T is a plateful of something, all yellow and white,
And she sings as she comes, with her smile so bright:
"'T is the best bread and butter I ever did see,
And it is for Alice's supper," says she.

THE BUMBLE-BEE.

The bumble-bee, the bumble-bee,
He flew to the top of the tulip-tree;
He flew to the top, but he could not stop,
For he had to get home to his early tea.

The bumble-bee, the bumble-bee,
He flew away from the tulip-tree;
But he made a mistake, and flew into the lake,
And he never got home to his early tea.

"LITTLE TOMMY TUCKER! SING FOR YOUR SUPPER."

THE ANIMALS OF BERNE.

By Pauline King.

I have a set of Animals
From Berne across the sea.
You'd never think that cows and pigs
So beautiful could be.

For all the pigs are pale light blue,
And all the cows are green;
Their coats are speckled o'er with flowers
Of every kind that's seen.

The horses are a fine bright pink
With daisies mottled over—
The cats are white and violet,
With leaves of meadow clover.

There are no animals like those
In all my Noah's Ark;
There are no animals like those
In all of Central Park.

And sometimes when I think of them
You don't know how I yearn
To see those lovely animals
A-walking round in Berne.

"IF WISHES WERE HORSES, THEN BEGGARS WOULD RIDE."

Allegro.

Old Gran-ger Grind whips out be-hind, and lets no-bod-y ride; But

SHOPPING

I've come to buy a frock to-day for my Matilda Jane,
(I think she's just a lovely doll, though father calls her plain!)
It must be something pretty; a kind of pink, or blue:
Yes, that is really very sweet: I think that it will do.
There's nothing more I want to-day. (I hope it's not too dear!)
Oh yes, I'll pay you for it now; I've got the money here.
Please wrap it up in paper and put it in the train.
Come, Baby dear, I think we must be getting home again.

W. W. Gibson.

"OH, MR. FAIRY, PLEASE."

Oh, Mr. Fairy, please
　Don't go away!
I am just a little girl
　Come out to play.

Just me, all by myself;
　Jack's gone to school.
You need n't hide away
　Behind that stool.

Oh, Mr. Fairy-man,
　Don't go away—
I 've heard of you before;
　Do come and play!

WISHES

BY FLORENCE E. PRATT.

A REGINALD BIRCH little boy
    Met the sweetest of Greenaway girls;
She, dressed all in Puritan brown,
    He, with cavalier ruffles and curls.

Her eyes were of solemnest brown,
    Her hair was cropped close to her head.
His curls were a riot of gold,
    His cheeks were of healthiest red.

They looked at each other awhile,
    Gay gallant and Puritan maid;
Then the Reginald Birch little boy
    Slowly and solemnly said:

"I wish *you* wore rufflety clothes!
    I wish that *my* hair was cut short!

'Cause the boys call me 'missy' and 'girl,'
And it interferes so with my sport."

Said she, "Oh, I like pretty clothes,
And I *do* wish they 'd let my hair curl!
I wish *you* were a Greenaway boy,
And I was a Fauntleroy girl!"

LITTLE MR. BY-AND-BY.

LITTLE Mr. By-and-By,
You will mark him by his cry,
And the way he loiters when
Called again and yet again,
Glum if he must leave his play
Though all time be holiday.

Little Mr. By-and-By,
Eyes cast down and mouth awry!
In the mountains of the moon
He is known as Pretty Soon;
And he 's cousin to Don't Care,
As no doubt you 're well aware.

Little Mr. By-and-By
Always has a fretful " Why ? "
When he 's asked to come or go,
Like his sister — Susan Slow.
Hope we 'll never — you nor I —
Be like Mr. By-and-By.
  Clinton Scollard.

Taking Dolly's Photograph

Ah, naughty Dolly! — When I say:
'Just turn a little more this way,
And then perhaps: 'Now, smile,' I find
You do not even try to mind.

"But when I say: 'Now, pet, keep still,'
I'm very, very sure you will,
And there's no need to say to you:
'Look pleasant' — for you always do."

PRACTISING SONG.

By Laura E. Richards.

Ri tum tiddy-iddy, ri tum tum!
Here I must sit for an hour and strum.
Practice is the thing for a good little girl,
It makes her nose straight, and it makes her hair curl.

Ri tum tiddy-iddy, ri tum ti!
Bang on the low notes and twiddle on the high.
Whether it's a jig or the "Dead March" in Saul,
I sometimes often feel as if I did n't care at all.

Ri tum tiddy-iddy, ri tum tee!
I don't mind the whole or the half note, you see.
It's the sixteenth and the quarter that confuse my mother's daughter,
And a thirty-second really is too dreadful to be taught her.

Ri tum tiddy-iddy, ri tum to!
I shall never, never, never learn the minor scale, I know.
It's gloomier and awfuller than puppy dogs a-howling,
And what's the use of practising such melancholy yowling?

But —*ri tum tiddy-iddy, ri tum tum!*
Still I work away with my drum, drum, drum.
For practi is good for a good little girl;
It makes her nose straight, and it makes her hair curl.*

* This last line is not true, little girls; but it is *so* hard, you know, to find good reasons for practising.

MAY-TIME IN THE COUNTRY.

THE FIELDS.

In summer-time I often go
Out to the fields where daisies grow
And, kneeling on the grassy ground,
I pick the flowers all around.

And just before I leave the field
I find a buttercup concealed
Down in the grass. And then I stay
To pluck its petals while I say:

"One for fingers, two for thumbs,
Three for cherries, four for plums,
And five for bread and butter nice;
I'll just go home and get a slice."

THE TIDES.

As once I played beside the sea,
Its waters gently came to me,
To bring me seaweed, stones, and shells,
And wash the sand where I dig wells.

But when I went another day,
The waters slowly flowed away,
To gather shells and pebbles more
For me to play with on the shore.

"I'LL GIVE YOUR BACK SUCH A SCRATCH AS YOU NEVER HAD IN ALL YOUR LIFE!" CRIED PUSS.

PUSSY AND THE TURTLE.

ONCE upon a time there lived a pretty little kitten. His mother was just beginning to teach him how to catch mice. So, one day, he stole away and went down into a cold cellar to go a-hunting all by himself. "I'll catch ever so many," he thought: "Six for mother, one for brother Spotty, one for Dotty, one for Scramble, one for Tumble, and two for poor little Flop who never is well."

Then he sat and waited. "It is the way to begin," he thought; "and I must be very quiet, like mother!" At this moment something stirred a pile of turnips in the corner, and the top one fell off and started to roll along the cellar floor.

Pussy flew upon it in a jiffy. "Good!" he exclaimed, "I've killed it — though it does n't seem to be a mouse. How cold and queer it feels! I wish Scramble was with me. Guess I'll go back to mother as soon as I've caught one real mouse."

Just then he heard a hard, thumping sound. With a start and a jump he turned quickly, and if there was n't a great big turtle creeping toward him! Turtles, you know, move very, very slowly. I suppose they find their hard shell rather heavy.

"Oh, dear! I don't want to catch any mouse at all," said Puss to himself. "I'm scared. I want to go back."

Still the turtle moved toward him, nearer and nearer. "Oh! oh!" thought Pussy, now afraid to move, "it's going to pounce upon me. I know it is. And if I run away he'll catch me, sure!"

The turtle came closer.

"Go 'way! go 'way!" cried Puss. "You just dare to touch me, and I'll give your back such a scratch as you never had in all your life!"

The turtle turned around and waddled slowly off.

"Now's my chance," cried Puss, and he jumped upon the enemy.

"The idea of that little puss trying to hurt my hard back!" said the turtle to himself, and he drew completely into his shell so that he might have a good laugh.

"Dear me!" thought puss in horror, "*where has his head gone to?* I must have bitten it off! What *will* mother say?"

And he scampered away, as fast as his legs could carry him, to tell Spotty, Dotty, Tumble, Scramble, and Flop, the wonderful news.

THE SECOND KITTEN'S HUNT.

"Mama," said another kitten, about a week after his brother's meeting with the turtle as was told in the last story. "I am grown up, and I should like to go and catch mice. I sha'n't catch a turtle."

"Why not wait a few weeks?" said his mother.

"I can't wait. I feel so big and strong, I must hunt," said the kitten.

"But do you know how?" his mother asked.

"It is easy," said the kitten. "All I have to do is to run after a mouse till I get him in a corner, and then put my paw on him."

"But mice are sly," said his mother. "So am I," said the kitten.

"Very well," said his mother; "and I hope you will catch one."

So the kitten walked away with his tail held up high, and went down into the cellar. The cellar was not very dark, and soon the kitten saw two rats come creeping and crawling out, to sup upon some wheat stalks which were in a corner near the big barrel. He thought they were mice. The kitten saw that there was a queer sort of box there, made of wires, but he did not know what it was. "It is a bird-cage," he said, "but some mean cat has eaten the bird already. Never mind, I will catch a mouse."

So the kitten jumped, and hit his paw very hard on the stone floor. But the rats jumped, too, and the kitten heard them laughing. So he was cross, and ran after one of the rats as hard as he could go.

Now, this was a clever rat, and he saw that the kitten did not know how to catch him. He ran about a little while, and then played he was very tired, and sat down near one end of the queer "bird-cage."

"Ah!" said the kitten, "I have tired him out; now I will jump on him."

So the kitten jumped!—away ran the rat, safe and sound, but there was a sharp click!—and the kitten found himself caught in the "bird-cage."

"Now, what would mama do, if she was in here?" said the kitten to himself. "I did not ask her how to get out of a bird-cage."

Just then the rats came up to the cage and, hearing him call it a "bird-cage," said:

"What a pretty bird! Sing, birdie, sing!"

A little rat peeked out from a hole in the wall, and said, "Tee-hee!"

The kitten was very glad when he heard his mother in soft, furry slippers, not long after, and he said, "Here I am, Mama — in the 'bird-cage'!"

"Bird-cage," said his mother, and then she began to laugh, too, and said, "Tee-hee," just as the rats had done. When she stopped laughing, she said:

"Why, Kit, that's a rat-trap! and I think you must be taught a little before you go hunting mice again." Then she helped him out.

As they went up-stairs the kitten heard the three rats in the cellar, and they said, "Tee-hee! Tee-hee! Tee-hee!"

KIT IN THE "BIRD CAGE."

THAT LITTLE GIRL

By Claude Harris.

I.

I OFTEN hear folks talking,
    a-laughing and a-talking
About a little girl who "lives
    not very far from here";
One who's "extremely mussy"
And "meddlesome" and "fussy,"
Who "loves to wander through the house and
    get things out of gear."
    I'm glad I'm not so mussy
    And meddlesome and fussy;
I cannot see why any girl can be so very queer.

II.

I've just heard mother joking, a-scolding and
    a-joking
About a little girl who "does not live a mile
    away."
    She says she is "a midget
    Made up of mostly fidget,"
And "from Monday until Sunday, she does
    nothing else but play."
    I'm glad I'm not "a midget
    Made up of mostly fidget."
I'm glad I'm not so little that I cannot quiet
    stay.

III.

I once heard Papa hinting, a-talking and a-
    hinting
About a little girl who "does n't live up in
    the moon."
    He says she's "very silly,
    And her first name is n't Billy,"
That she "talks the blessed morning, if she
    does n't sleep till noon."
    I'm glad I am not silly,
    Though my first name is n't Billy,
And I hardly ever talk at all, and always "get
    up soon."

IV.

I've heard some folks complaining, a-sighing
    and complaining,
About a little girl who lives "next door to folks
    they know."
    They say she's "very lazy,"
    She "almost sets them crazy,"
That she's "always doing nothing, and does it
    very slow."
    I'm glad I am not lazy,
    I never set folks crazy,
And I work so very very much I've hardly
    time to grow.

The Popular Poplar Tree.

A Song for Margaret and Harold.

BY BLANCHE WILLIS HOWARD.

WHEN the great wind sets things whirling
   And rattles the window-panes,
And blows the dust in giants
   And dragons tossing their manes;
When the willows have waves like water,
   And children are shouting with glee;
When the pines are alive and the larches,
   Then hurrah for you and me,
     In the tip o' the top o' the top o' the tip of
       the popular poplar tree!

Don't talk about Jack and the Beanstalk!
   He did not climb half so high!
And Alice in all her travels
   Was never so near the sky!
Only the swallow, a-skimming
   The storm-cloud over the lea,
Knows how it feels to be flying —
   When the gusts come strong and free —
     In the tip o' the top o' the top o' the tip of
       the popular poplar tree!

"Cock-a-doodle-doo!
My Dame has lost her shoe,
Master broke his fiddling-stick
And don't know what to do."

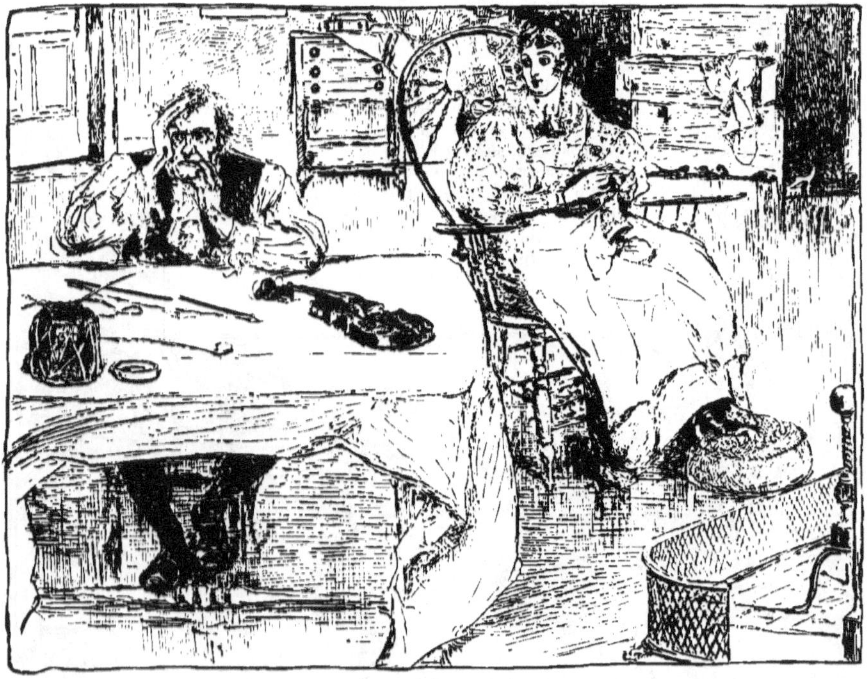

THE BUMBLE-BEE AND THE GRASSHOPPER.

A BUMBLE-BEE, yellow as gold,
   Sat perched on a red-clover top,
When a grasshopper, wiry and old,
   Came along with a skip and a hop.
"Good-morrow!" cried he, "Mr. Bumble-Bee!
You seem to have come to a stop."

"We people that work,"
   Said the bee with a jerk,
"Find a benefit sometimes in stopping;
   Only insects like you,
   Who have nothing to do,
Can keep up a perpetual hopping."

The grasshopper paused on his way,
   And thoughtfully hunched up his knees;
"Why trouble this sunshiny day,"
   Quoth he, "with reflections like these?
I follow the trade for which I was made;
We all can't be wise bumble-bees.

"There's a time to be sad,
   And a time to be glad;
A time both for working and stopping;
   For men to make money,
   For you to make honey,
And for me to do nothing but hopping."

SOMETHING BETWEEN A GOOSE AND A PEACOCK.

THE SCISSORS
BY LAURA E. RICHARDS

WE 'RE a jolly pair of twins,
   And we always work together.
We are always bright and sharp,
   However dull the weather.
Whenever little Maidie
   Takes her work-box in her lap,
We are always up and ready
   With our "Snip, snip, snap!"

We cut the dolly's mantle;
   We shape the dolly's dress.
Oh, half the clever things we do
   You 'd never, never guess!
For food or sleep or playtime
   We do not care a rap,
But are ready, night and daytime,
   With our "Snip, snip, snap!"

The Needle

IN and out, in and out
   Goes my shining way.
Never stop for round about,
   Put it through, I say.

Push along, push along,
   Neighbor Thimble, do;
Though I 'm bright and stout and strong,
   I have need of you.

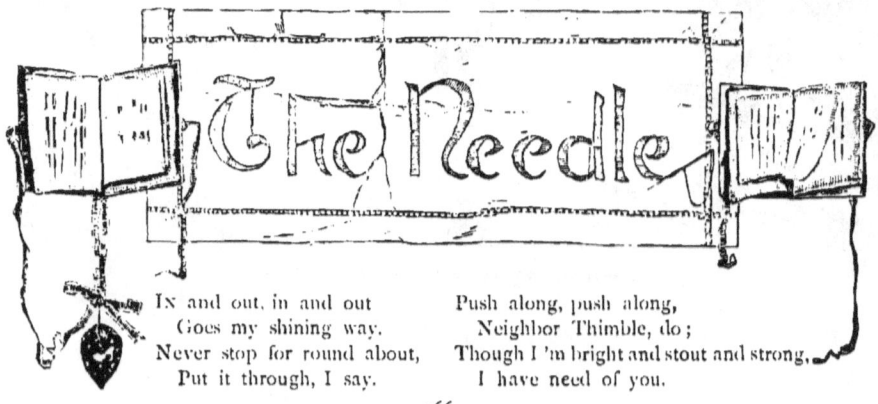

I 've a *stitch* in my side,
   Hem in my throat;
I have to *run*
   Like a mountain goat.
I *fell*, but never a hurt got I;
   And merrily sounds my *gathering*-cry.

In and out, in and out,
   Goes my shining way;
I shall do, beyond a doubt,
   All my work to-day.

Follow me, follow me,
   Neighbor Thread, now do;
Though I 'm clever, you can see
   I have need of you.

The Thread.

By Laura E. Richards

Brother Needle goes a-flashing,
   Goes a-darting and a-dashing,
   Out and in, and in and out
   Catching everything about.

After him I slip along,
Make things snug and fast and strong.
Without bragging, I may be
Quite as *need(le)*ful as he.

Never make a kink in me;
Careless sewing that would be.
Keep me clean, nor leave a track
Where I pass, of gray or black.

Little fingers quick and light,
See that you are clean and white.
Do your part, and me you 'll find
Smooth to slip and safe to bind.

THE THIMBLE

"FINGER-HAT."

LITTLE finger, slim and nimble,
Here am I, your friendly Thimble.
(Germans call me "Finger-hat";
Jolly little name is that.)
Put me on, and you will see
What a helper I can be.
Brother Needle's very fine —
Sharp and clever, in his line,
But he oft would puzzled be,
If he had no help from me!

THE STORY OF MOTHER HUBBARD, TOLD IN JAPANESE PICTURES.

Across the flowing river,
On a pretty little hill,
There rests a little city,
And a busy little mill.

And everything that goes that way
Doth small and smaller grow,—
The people on the long curved bridge.
The boats that move so slow.

I am sure that in the little streets
A tiny people walk;
I am sure that everything is neat
And small, and clean as chalk.

And some day I will go there, too,
And live in a tiny house;
And own, perhaps, a little horse
No bigger than a mouse.

But not for some time yet; because
A girl one moonlight night
Started, and while we watched her
She went right out of sight!
Elizabeth Chase.

In Japan

by Juliet Wilbor Tompkins

"Come, little pigeon, all weary with play,
Come and thy pinions furl."
That's what a Japanese mother would say
To her dear little Japanese girl.
"Cease to flutter thy white, white wings,
Now that the day is dead.
Listen and dream while the mother-bird sings".
That means, "It's time for bed."

"Stay, little sunbeam, and cherish me here:
My heart is so cold when you roam."
That is the Japanese—"No, my dear;
I'd rather you played at home."
"Roses and lilies shall strew thy way:
The Sun-Goddess now has smiled".
That's what a Japanese mother would say
To a good little Japanese child.

THE GREAT BICYCLE RACE AT GRASSHOPPERTOWN — THE START.

THE FINISH — A SURPRISE.

A REAL UNCLE REMUS STORY.

JINGLES.

By John Kendrick Bangs.

I. A PUZZLER.

My papa is a great big man;
  But what I cannot see is
Just how they're going to work that plan
  To make me big as he is.

II. A CURIOUS DISCOVERY.

My brother's brother's not my brother;
  And this is why, you see,
Though his dear mother's *my* dear mother,
  My brother's brother's me.

A YANKEE NAPOLEON: "BRING ON YOUR DUKE OF WELLINGTON."

A RACE IN THE AIR.

QUITE A HISTORY.
(After the German.)

BY ARLO BATES.

"Where have you been, Lysander Pratt?"
"In Greedy Land, Philander Sprat."
"What did you there to grow so fat?"

"I built myself a little house
  In which I lived snug as a mouse."

"Well, very, very good was that!"
"Not wholly good, Philander Sprat."
"Now wherefore not, Lysander Pratt?"

"A bear came raging from the wood,
  And tumbled down my cottage good."

"Alas! how very bad was that!"
"Not wholly bad, Philander Sprat."
"Not bad? Why not, Lysander Pratt?'

"I killed the bear, and of his skin
  I made a coat to wrap me in."

"Well done! Now surely good was that."
"Yet not so good, Philander Sprat."
"Now, why not good, Lysander Pratt?"

"A wicked hound tore up my coat
  Until it was not worth a groat."

"Ah, what an evil thing was that!"
"Not wholly bad, Philander Sprat."
"What good was there, Lysander Pratt?"

"He caught for me a great wild boar,
 That made me sausages good store."

"What luck! How very good was that!"
"Good? Not all good, Philander Sprat."
"Why not all good, Lysander Pratt?"

"A cat stole in on velvet paw,
 And ate them all with greedy maw."

"Now surely wholly bad was that!"
"Not wholly bad, Philander Sprat."
"Then tell me why, Lysander Pratt."

"Of pussy's fur with silken hair,
 I made of gloves a noble pair."

"Trust you! No wonder you are fat!
 You found your good account in that
 As in all else, Lysander Pratt."

"Yes, in the closet hang they now.
 Yet they are full of holes, I vow,

"Gnawed by some thievish long-tailed rat.
 And so, you see, Philander Sprat,
 Not wholly good was even that!"

"LOOK OUT, THERE!"

A LITTLE girl one day in the month of May dropped a morning-glory seed into a small hole in the ground and said: "Now, Morning-glory Seed, hurry and grow, grow, grow until you are a tall vine covered with pretty green leaves, and lovely trumpet-flowers." But the earth was very dry, for there had been no rain for a long time, and the poor wee seed could not grow at all. So, after lying patiently in the small hole for nine long days and nine long nights, it said to the ground around it: "O Ground, please give me a few drops of water to soften my hard brown coat, so that it may burst open and set free my two green seed-leaves, and then I can begin to be a vine!" But the ground said: "That you must ask of the rain."

So the seed called to the rain: "O Rain, please come down and wet the ground around me so that it may give me a few drops of water. Then will my hard brown coat grow softer and softer until at last it can burst open and set free my two green seed-leaves and I can begin to be a vine!" But the rain said: "I can not unless the clouds hang lower."

So the seed called to the clouds: "O Clouds, please hang lower and let the rain come down and wet the ground around me, so that it may give me a few drops of water. Then will my hard brown coat grow softer and softer until at last it can burst open and set free my two green seed-leaves and I can begin to be a vine!" But the clouds said: "The sun must hide, first."

So the seed called to the sun: "O Sun, please hide for a little while so that the clouds may hang lower, and the rain come down and wet the ground around me. Then will the ground give me a few drops of water and my hard brown coat grow softer and softer until at last it can burst open and set free my two green seed-leaves and I can begin to be a vine!" "I will," said the sun; and he was gone in a flash.

Then the clouds began to hang lower and lower, and the rain began to fall faster and faster, and the ground began to get wetter and wetter, and the seed-coat began to grow softer and softer until at last open it burst!—and out came two bright green seed-leaves and the Morning-glory Seed began to be a Vine!

CIRCUS ELEPHANTS HAVING A GOOD TIME BY THEMSELVES.

THE CIRCUS ELEPHANT'S SATURDAY-NIGHT BATH.

UP IN A BALLOON.

We all went up in a big balloon—
  Father, Uncle, Freddy, and I;
The band struck up a beautiful tune,
  And all the populace waved "good-
    bye."

At first it wavered, and jerked, and
    swayed,
And father asked: "Do you feel
    afraid?"
    But I laughed: "Oh, no,
    It is grand to go;"
And so he called me his brave little
    maid.

Up we went! oh, ever so high!
Up, till we must have touched the
    sky.
    Town, river, and bay,
    All faded away,—
And then poor Freddy began to cry;
"I want to get out," he screamed;
    "oh, my!"

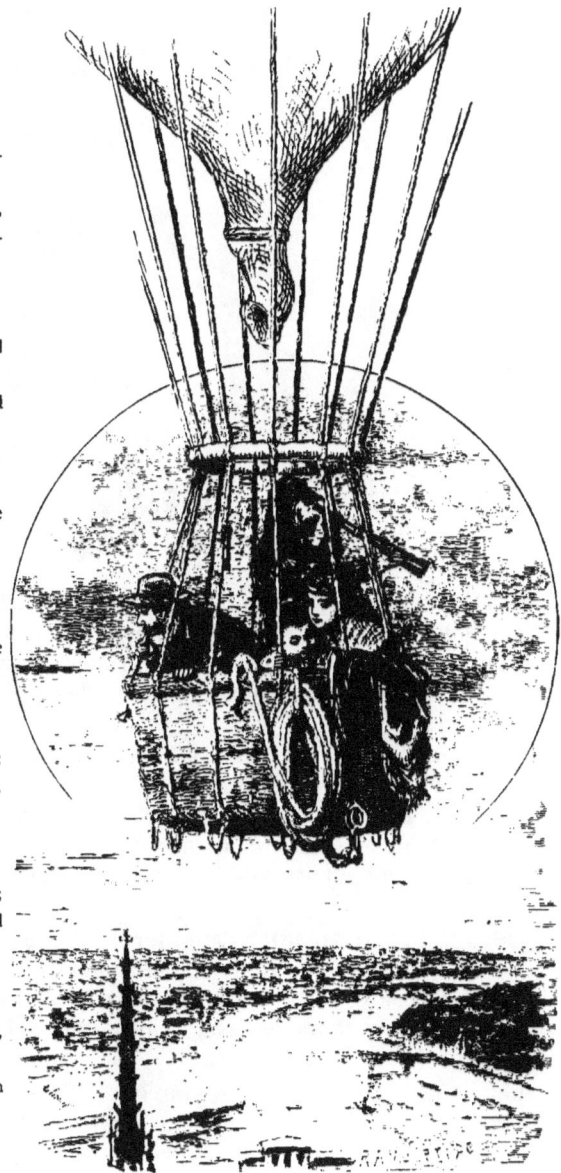

Up, up, we went, and on we sailed;
While still poor Freddy wept and
    wailed.
    He jumped about,
    And tried to get out;
And so we soon went down, down,
    down,
And tied the balloon to a tree in
    town.

THE DEAD DOLL.

By Margaret Vandegrift.

You need n't be trying to comfort me — I tell you my dolly is dead!
There's no use saying she is n't, with a crack like that in her head.
It's just like you said it would n't hurt much to have my tooth out that day;
And then, when the man 'most pulled my head off, you had n't a word to say.

And I guess you must think I'm a baby, when you say you can mend it with glue!
As if I did n't know better than that! Why, just suppose it was you.
You might make her *look* all mended; but what do I care for looks?
Why, glue's for chairs and tables, and toys, and the backs of books!

My dolly! My own little daughter! Oh, but it's the awfulest crack!
It just makes me sick to think of the sound when her poor head went whack
Against that horrible brass thing that holds up the little shelf.
Now, Nursey, what makes you remind me? I know that I did it myself!

I think you must be crazy — you 'll get her another head!
What good would forty heads do her? I tell you my dolly is dead!
And to think I had n't quite finished her elegant new Spring hat!
And I took a sweet ribbon of hers last night to tie on that horrid **cat!**

When my Mamma gave me that ribbon — I was playing out in the yard —
She said to me, most expressly, "Here's a ribbon for Hildegarde."
And I went and put it on Tabby, and Hildegarde saw me do it;
But I said to myself, "Oh, never mind, I don't believe she knew it!"

But I know that she knew it now, and I just believe, I do,
That her poor little heart was broken, and so her head broke too.
Oh, my baby! my little baby! I wish *my* head had been hit!
For I've hit it over and over, and it has n't cracked a bit.

But since the darling *is* dead, she'll want to be buried, of course;
We will take my little wagon, Nurse, and you shall be the horse;
And I'll walk behind and cry; and we'll put her in this, you see —
This dear little box — and we'll bury her then under the maple-tree.

And Papa will make a tombstone, like the one he made for my bird;
And he'll put what I tell him on it — yes, every single word!
I shall say: "Here lies Hildegarde, a beautiful doll, who is dead;
She died of a broken heart, and a dreadful crack in her head."

THE LAND OF NODDY.

Put away the bauble and the bib,
Smooth out the pillows in the crib,
   Softly on the down
   Lay the baby's crown,
   Warm around its feet
   Tuck the little sheet, —
Snug as a pea in a pod!
   With a yawn and a gap,
   And a dreamy little nap,
     We will go, we will go,
To the Landy-andy-pandy
Of Noddy-oddy-poddy,
   To the Landy-andy-pand
     Of Noddy-pod.

Then when the morning breaks,
Then when the lark awakes,
   We will leave the drowsy dreams,
   And the twinkling starry gleams:
   Leave the Shadow-maker's tent,
   And the wonders in it pent,
To return to our own native sod.
   With a hop and a skip,
   And a jump and a flip,
     We will come, we will come,
From the Landy-andy-pandy
Of Noddy-oddy-poddy,
   From the Landy-andy-pand
     Of Noddy-pod.

THE CITY CHILD.
By Alfred Tennyson.

DAINTY little maiden, whither would you wander?
    Whither from this pretty home, the home where mother dwells?
"Far and far away," said the dainty little maiden,
"All among the gardens, auriculas, anemones,
    Roses and lilies and Canterbury-bells."

Dainty little maiden, whither would you wander?
    Whither from this pretty house, this city-house of ours?
"Far and far away," said the dainty little maiden,
"All among the meadows, the clover and the clematis,
    Daisies and kingcups and honeysuckle-flowers."

DOWN IN THE MEADOW.
By Ruth Hall.

DOWN in the meadow-land, far and fair,
I met, this morning, sweet Silverhair.
"What do you here?" I asked the small rover.
"Oh, I am seeking a four-leaved clover!"

"What will that do for you, little one?"
"Give me all good things under the sun,—
Not me, only, but Mother, moreover:
That's why I look for a four-leaved clover!"

Wild red strawberries sent their sweetness;
Gay young butterflies tried their fleetness;
All things courted the grave little rover.
Silverhair looked for a four-leaved clover.

Still was the garden yon hedge incloses;
When something suddenly stirred the roses;—
Happy the cry of the dear little rover:
"Mother! I've brought you a four-leaved clover!"

CRADLE SONG.

By Margaret Johnson.

To and fro,
So soft and slow,
Swingeth the baby's cradle O!
Still he lies
With laughing eyes,
And will not into Dream-land go.

Lullaby!
The crickets cry,
The twinkling stars are in the sky.
Soft dews fall,
While robins call,
And homeward swift the swallows fly.

Sleep, oh, sleep!
In slumber deep.
Sweet dreams across thine eyes shall creep,
And all night
The soft moonlight
Within thy curtained cradle peep.

Hush! he sighs—
The laughter flies
All swiftly from his drowsy eyes.
To and fro,
More soft—more slow—
And fast asleep the baby lies.

"HE HAD ONE BIG BOAT AND HE MADE A FLAG FOR IT HIMSELF"

BENNY AND HIS BOATS.

By M. L. B. Branch.

BENNY was a little boy who lived by a river that ran into the great ocean, and he liked to sail boats so well that his father made him six, all of a size, with a boom and a gaff and two sails apiece. He had one big boat, too, and he made a flag for it himself. His six little boats were named "Pearl," "Phœbe," "Dolphin," "Star," "Racer," and "Kate."

Now, there was a great time in Benny's family, for grandpa, who lived away out west, and who had a ranch there, had written to them to come and join him, and help him raise sheep and horses. So they began to pack up their things; but, as they could not take all, they sold some, and some they gave away. Papa told Benny he had better give his boats to his playmates.

"Why, no," said Benny; "I can't do without my boats! I'll give the boys my checkers and my ninepins, but I can't give away my boats! I love my boats!"

And, with his mama's help, he packed them the next day carefully in a box.

"There isn't even a brook on the ranch!" papa said to mama; "and all the water has to be pumped with windmills."

"Never mind," she replied. "Benny has to leave the sea he loves, but he shall not leave his boats. It may make him happy to look at them."

In another month the little family reached the far-off ranch, and Benny was very happy. He had a pony to ride upon, and a dog to follow him.

"Do you like it here, Benny?" asked grandpa, at the end of three weeks.

"Yes, grandpa, I do," said Benny. "All I want now is a brook."

And then he told his grandpa that he had brought six boats named Pearl, Phœbe, Dolphin, Star, Racer, and Kate.

Grandpa whistled, and then he laughed. "We must sail them!" he exclaimed.

"But there is no water," said Benny.

"Water does not sail boats," said grandpa. "No, the wind does that," Benny said.

Grandpa now went to work and made a frame with six arms, and on each arm he fastened a boat, and then he went up on a ladder to the top of the barn. When he came down from the ladder, a little breeze was filling the sails, and the boats were moving around and around. By and by it blew harder, and the boats moved faster. Benny shouted for joy, and called everybody to see.

So now the boats had a place where they could sail east, west, south, north, and many a time they went so fast that nobody could tell, not even Benny, which was Pearl, or which was Phœbe, or which was Dolphin, or Star, or Racer, or Kate.

"THE BOATS COULD SAIL EAST, WEST, SOUTH AND NORTH."

A FAIRY GODMOTHER.

By Mary Bradley.

"Oh, dearie me!" one morning sighed our merry little Lou,
"I have n't got a single thing — a single thing to do!
I wish a fairy-godmother would come and talk with me,
And let me wish three wishes; I wonder what they 'd be?

"Well, first, — now let me think a while, — I 'd wish for bags of gold;
A hundred million dollars I guess I 'd make them hold.
And then I 'd wish for golden hair, and beautiful blue eyes,
And a real grown-up lover to praise me to the skies;
I 'd wish — oh, yes! to be a queen, and he should be the king,
With courtiers, and trumpeters, and all that sort of thing.
We 'd ride on milk-white palfreys all dressed in gold and green,
And the people everywhere would shout, 'Long live our gracious Queen!'
Oh, would n't it be lovely?" sighed foolish little Lou;
"I wish the fairy-godmother was here, and it was true."

Just then her own real mother called: "Oh, Lulu, child, come here!
I wish you 'd rock the baby a little while, my dear.
He 's dropping off to sleep, you see, — he 'll soon be quiet now.
And then I wish you 'd shell the peas, while Bridget milks the cow.
She says she 's 'clane bewildered' to know which way to turn,
For Sandy 's in the mowing-field, and Nora 's got to churn:
I wish you 'd set the table, and see what you can do
To help us with the little things — that 's mother's daughter Lou!"

Up jumped the little maiden, with a twinkle in her eyes,
And a merry notion in her head both whimsical and wise:
"My mother wished three wishes! Now I shall have the fun
Of being fairy-godmother, and granting every one."

As cheery as a cricket she went about all day,
And out of every little task she made a sort of play,
Until her happy laughter, and the tuneful song she sung
Had sweetened Bridget's temper, and stopped her fretting tongue.
The baby, too, she humored in many a baby whim;
He cried for her at bed-time to go up-stairs with him;
And her mother kissed her fondly when she found her nodding there,
With his chubby fingers tangled in his sister's curly hair.

"You 've been my comfort-daughter this livelong day," she said;
But Lulu hardly understood — the little sleepy-head!
"It was such fun," she murmured, in a dreamy, drowsy way,
"To be a fairy-godmother! I 've had a *lovely* day."

THE GREEDY TOAD.

By Eliza S. Turner.

Down in the long grass, as snug as a mole,
He called from his little h, o, l, e, hole:
"Oh, Ma, have you any m, e, a, t, meat?
I seem to want something to e, a, t, eat."

"Then out with your tongue, and t, r, y, try
To capture a bug or an f, l, y, fly."

"Oh, I won't have a bug, or such t, o, y, toy.
I want bread and meat like a b, o, y, boy.
No, I won't have a fly nor a b, u, g, bug,
But m i, l, k, milk from a j, u, g, jug."

"A t, o. a, d, want m, i, l. k, milk?
You'll next want a coat of s, i, l, k, silk!

You're losing your w, i, t, s, wits!"
And she laughed herself into f, i, t, s, fits.

But still he cried out: "I shall d, i, e, die,
If I don't get some milk and some p, i, e, pie.'

"Here, take it," she cried in a p, e, t, pet;
"And sick enough of it you'll g, e, t, get."
And oh, at his first l, i, c, k, lick,
He found himself growing s, i, c, k, sick.
And still, as he ate like a p, i, g, pig,
He seemed to be swelling too b, i, g, big;
And over the milk — it's t, r, u, e, true —
He choked himself almost b, l, u, e, blue:
And at the sixth quarter of p, i, e, pie,
He looked just as if he should d, i, e, die.
And soon he called out: "B, r, e, a, d, bread,"
And shouted: "I'm almost d, e, a, d, dead."

Said she: "I was right, you f, i, n, d, find;
Now next time perhaps you'll m, i, n, d mind."

THE BUMBLEBEES.

Down behind the garden wall, near the apple-trees,
"Z-z-z-z!" sing the bumblebees.
"Z-z-z-z!" This is what they say —
"Z-z-z-z!" — all the sunny day.
When they go into their nest, burly bumblebees,
'T is so very still then near the apple-trees.

On the Road to London Town

By E. M. Winston.

On the road to London town!
    We made an early start:
As soon as morning dawned I put
    The old gray to the cart.

My good wife Joan the breakfast got,
    And dressed the baby, too;
So now we 're dashing on to town,—
    Oh, don't you wish 't was you?

DOT AND THE NEW MOON.

I have been told — do you think it is true? —
That when the new moon first comes into
    view,
The bright little moon, like a bent silver bow,
If I see it just over my left shoulder — *so*,
Bad luck will follow me all the month through;
But I don't believe much in signs. Do you?

But the new moon, last night, above the elm-tree,
Over my *right* shoulder glanced down at me,
The pretty new moon, and, you know, that 's
    a sign
That the best of good luck will surely be mine.
I can't help believing *that* sign will come true.
Signs may be silly — but, now, would n't you?

A Family Drum Corps

By Malcolm Douglas.

A LITTLE man bought him a big bass-drum;
    Boom — boom — boom!
"Who knows," said he, "when a war will come?"
    Boom — boom — boom!
"I'm not at all frightened, you understand,
But, if I am called on to fight for my land,
I want to be ready to play in the band."
    Boom — boom — boom!

He got all his children little snare-drums;
    Boom — tidera-da — boom!
And they'd practise as soon as they'd finished their sums.
    Boom — tidera-da — boom!
"We're just like our papa," in chorus said they,
"And, if we should ever get into the fray,
Why, it's safer to thump than to fight any day!"
    Boom — tidera-da — boom!

And, showing her spirit, the little man's wife —
    Boom — tidera-da — boom!
With some of her pin-money purchased a fife;
    Boom — tidera-da — boom!
And, picking out tunes that were not very hard,
They'd play them while marching around the back yard,
Without for one's feelings the slightest regard.
    Boom — tidera-da — boom-a-diddle-dee —
    Boom — tidera-da — boom!

The little old parson, who lived next door —
    Boom — tidera-da — boom!
Would throw up his hands, as he walked the floor;
    Boom — tidera-da — boom!
"Won't you stop it, I beg you?" he often said.
"I'm trying to think of a text, but instead
The only thing I can get into my head
    Is your boom — tidera-da — boom-a-diddle-dee —
    Boom — tidera-da — boom!"

And all of the people, for blocks around —
    Boom — tidera-da — boom!
Kept time at their tasks to the martial sound;
    Boom — tidera-da — boom!
While children to windows and stoops would fly,
Expecting to see a procession pass by,
And they could n't make out why it never drew nigh,
    With its boom — tidera-da — boom-a-diddle-dee —
    Boom — tidera-da — boom!

It would seem such vigor must soon abate;
    Boom — tidera-da — boom!
But they still keep at it, early and late;
    Boom — tidera-da — boom!
So, if it should be that a war breaks out,
They 'll all be ready, I have no doubt,
To help in putting the foe to rout,
    With their boom — tidera-da — boom —
    Boom — tidera-da — Boom —
    Boom — tidera-da — boom-a-diddle-dee —
    Boom — BOOM — BOOM!

Christmas Verses.

A New Mother Goose Jingle.

Sing a song of Christmas-time,
Mistletoe and holly,
Two impatient little girls,
Genevieve and Dolly.
When the door was opened
They shouted in their glee,
And wouldn't you have shouted too
To have so fine a tree?

Dorothy G. Rice

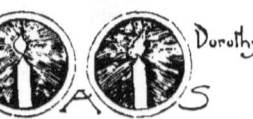

MERRY CHRISTMAS.

M for the **M**usic, merry and clear;
E for the **E**ve, the crown of the year.
R for the **R**omping of bright girls and boys;
R for the **R**eindeer that bring them the toys;
Y for the **Y**ule-log softly aglow.

C for the **C**old of the sky and the snow;
H for the **H**earth where they hang up the hose;
R for the **R**eel which the old folks propose.
I for the **I**cicles seen through the pane;
S for the **S**leigh-bells, with tinkling refrain.
T for the **T**ree with gifts all abloom;
M for the **M**istletoe hung in the room;
A for the **A**nthems we all love to hear;
S for **S**t **N**icholas — joy of the year!

THE BEST TREE.

BY JANET S. ROBERTSON.

KARL lay on the floor by the
    firelight bright
  Thinking about the trees.
"I love them all," he said to himself,
  As he named them over with ease;
"The chestnut, ash, and oak so high,
  The pine with its needle leaves,
The spruce, and cedar, and hemlock green,
  And the maple with its keys.

"The dainty willow with pussies gray,
  The birch with bark so white,
The apple-tree with its blossoms sweet,
  And the fruit so red and bright.
But the one I love the *best* of all
  Blooms and bears fruit together;
It is sure to be filled at this time of the year,
  Whatever may be the weather.

"Its blossoms are blue and yellow and red,
  All shining with silvery hue.
There are stems of golden and silver thread,
  And candles that glisten like dew.
With such wonderful fruit there's none can compare;
  From lowest to topmost bough
Every sort of a toy is swinging in air—
  Jumping frogs, and cats that 'me-ow.'

"There are trumpets, and balls, and dolls
    that talk,
  And drums, and whistles that blow,
  And guns, and whips, and horses that walk,
  And books; and wagons that go.
There are musical tops, and boats that sail,
  And puzzles, and knives, and games;
There are Noah's arks, and also a whale,
  And boxes, and ribbons, and reins.

"There 's candy and oranges, skates and sleds,
  And mugs for good little girls,
  And cradles, and clothes for dollies' beds,
  And dolls with hair in curls.

There are fans for girls and tools for
    boys,
  And handkerchiefs, rattles, and ties,
  And horns, and bells, and such-like toys,
  And tea-sets and candy pies.

"Oh! what a sight is this wonderful tree,
  With its gifts that sparkle and hide!
Other trees may be good, but there 's none
    for me
Like the beautiful merry Christmas-tree
  With its branches spreading wide,—
  The merry, beautiful, sparkling tree
    That blossoms at Christmas-tide."

SANTA CLAUS STREET IN JINGLETOWN.

By Sarah J. Burke.

EVERY night when the lamps are lit,
   And the stars through the curtain begin to peep —
When pussy has grown too tired to play,
   And has laid herself down on the rug to sleep —
When the spoon drops into the empty bowl
   (For baby has eaten her bread and milk),
And bright eyes hide behind drooping lids,
   Fringed with lashes as soft as silk —
When I lift my baby and fold her bib,
And carry her off to her little crib,
She whispers: "Before we cuddle down
Let us take a journey to Jingletown."

Oh, Jingletown is a wonderful town!
   Mother Goose lives on its finest square,
And little Jack Horner bought his pie
   At one of the bakers' shops there.
The House that Jack Built stands near the church
Where they sounded Cock Robin's knell,
And Little Bo Peep there lost her sheep,
   When she took them to town to sell.
But the funniest thing of all is this —
You must stop at the toll-gate and pay a kiss!
For the tiniest tear or the slightest frown
Will keep a child out of Jingletown.

When we go, I follow my baby's lead,
   But, oh! she never wants to rest,
And I walk the streets of the queer old town
   In a never-ending quest.
But the street that my darling loves the most
   Is bordered with trees of evergreen,
Whose branches droop to the ground, and show
   The twinkling lights between.
There the merriest children swarm,
And my darling lingers, wrapped up warm
In her traveling robe of eider-down —
Santa Claus street, in Jingletown!

IF YOU 'RE GOOD.

By James Courtney Challiss.

SANTA CLAUS 'll come to-night,
   If you 're *good*,
And do what you know is right,
   As you should;
Down the chimney he will creep,
Bringing you a woolly sheep,
And a doll that goes to sleep; —
   If you 're *good*.

Santa Claus will drive his sleigh
   Thro' the wood,
But he 'll come around this way
   If you 're good,
With a wind-up bird that sings,
And a puzzle made of rings —
Jumping-jacks and funny things —
   If you 're *good*.

He will bring you cars that "go,"
   If you 're *good*,
And a rocking-horsey — *oh!*
   If he would!
And a dolly, if you please,
That says "Mama!" when you squeeze
It — he 'll bring you one of these,
   If you 're *good*.

Santa grieves when you are bad,
   As he should;
But it makes him very glad
   When you 're good.
He is wise, and he 's a dear;
Just do right and never fear;
He 'll remember you each year,
   If you 're *good*.

"THEY DANCED THEM A MEASURE ON CHRISTMAS NIGHT."

THE PICTURE.

BY MARY MAPES DODGE.

A LITTLE lady, a very young knight,—
Oh, their smiling faces were clear and bright,
Gold and laces and pearls had she,
And he was as fine as a lad could be.
They lived long ago, and their hearts were light,
As they danced them a measure on Christmas night.

But girls and boys, young, merry, and fair,
Gladden our firesides everywhere.
They thrive and flourish to-day, as then —
The little ladies, the little men!
And, grand or humble, their hearts are light
When they tread them a measure on Christmas night.

Goodnight!

www.ingramcontent.com/pod-product-compliance
Lightning Source LLC
Chambersburg PA
CBHW020815230426
43666CB00007B/1020